No Canadian Experience, Eh?

A Career Success Guide for New Immigrants

Daisy Wright

Printed in the USA

For information on book purchases please write WCS Publishers, 164 Sandalwood Parkway East, Suite 211, P.O. Box 1026, Brampton, ON, L6Z 4X1

ISBN 978-0-9813104-0-4

Library and Archives Canada Cataloguing in Publication

Wright, Daisy
        No Canadian experience, eh? : a career success guide for new immigrants / by Daisy Wright. -- 2nd ed.

Includes bibliographical references and index.
ISBN 978-0-9813104-0-4

        1. Job hunting--Canada--Handbooks, manuals, etc.
2. Immigrants--Employment--Canada--Handbooks, manuals, etc.
I. Title.

HF5382.75.C3W75 2011   650.14086'9120971   C2011-900437-2

DEDICATION

Dedicated to the memories of my dearest Mama, Edna Wallace, who passed away just before the second edition was completed

My wonderful niece, Sonia Richardson, whose generosity was limitless and who taught me the real meaning of faith.

My dear friend Gwen Howlett whose encouraging words I miss,

and

My Aunt Elsie (Solomon), my first kindergarten teacher who always believed in me.

TABLE OF CONTENTS

ACKNOWLEDGEMENTS

Renowned author Jack Canfield said we should celebrate our successes and express our gratitude to everyone who has helped us along the way. While it is impossible to acknowledge everyone who gave me words of advice and encouragement, especially as I juggled the tasks of being a self-published author, there are several individuals that deserve special mention.

- My immediate family who finally understood what kept me up all those late nights. Patrick, my other half, who supported me at every step of the way, allowed me to include his experiences in the book and wherever I speak, and most of all, encouraged me when the going got rough. Damali and Guion, our wonderful daughter and son, who gave me the space I needed and never complained when I said I was busy, because they knew what I was trying to achieve, My adoring grandson, Dakari, who arrived a year after the first edition and found ways to interrupt me at just the times I needed a break.

- My dearest mother, Edna, for her special prayers for me and this project. Sister Madge, Neville, Lorna, Herschel (Phonse), Mary, Cleveland (Sonny), Lascelles, Paulette, Sean, Diana, Donna-Dene, Kimone, Keneisha, Freddie, Nikki, Tanya, Simone, Dwayne, Krystal, Mercedes, Roxanne and Christian, Aunt Rossi, and my many other family members who kept telling me that it could be done.

- Those who provided support in our transition. My mother-in-law Pearleta, and the 'Wright' clan who were there at the beginning of our journey; Gladwin Hall and Fay Campbell who were our anchors on our arrival; and Janette Keene, and Yvette and Sel Smart who helped to make our move that much easier.

- My Master Mind Alliance team, (Denise Ricketts-Goombs, Elizabeth Allen, Jackie Palmer, Maureen Maragh, Sandy Richards and Sonia Shirley), who provided me with invaluable advice and suggestions.

- My Research & Development team – some of the most recognized career professionals around, and whose individual expertise has contributed to a richer edition. I owe them a debt of gratitude. See the 'List of Contributors' page for their contact details.

- My childhood friend, Norma Hodgson, whose words of wisdom provided encouragement, and Arlene Sukhu, my Ryerson batch-mate and friend whose research skills came in handy this time around.

- Dawn Martin, Marjorie Taylor and Hyacinth Campbell for their individual behind-the-scenes support, David & Inez Ayres for photography services during my first book signing at Chapters.

- Jasmine Sahoye and Alysia Moulton-White for media coverage in Canada and Jamaica, respectively, Wanda Marsman who provided valuable feedback, and Marguerite Orane for some helpful suggestions with this edition.

- Judeen, for Internet assistance during a visit to Jamaica, which enabled me to keep on schedule with editing and proofreading. Special thanks also to Lynda Margaret Reeves and Denise Ricketts-Goombs for their keen proofreading eyes.

- My editor, Angela Carter, for her patience and professionalism. Her background as a journalist and communication specialist made my job easier.

- Conestoga College for giving me the start through their Career Development Practitioner Program, and for recently honouring me with one of their **"2011 Alumni of Distinction"** Awards.
- Tyler Forkes, Executive Director for Alumni Relations at Ryerson University, adding a copy of the first edition to the Alumni Library.

- The Toronto Chapter of Holmwood Past Students Association, who gave me an award for outstanding achievement as a Holmwood Alumni.

- Colleagues of Career Professionals of Canada who twice honoured me as Outstanding Canadian Career Leader.

- Ingrid Norrish, my marketing coach and one of the most generous persons I know.

- Marni Johnson, President of Workplace Communication & Diversity Inc. for promoting the book wherever and whenever she gets a chance.

- Rossina Ippolito, for her tedious work and quick turnaround in creating the Index.

- The many people who freely shared their experiences; those who permitted me to include their stories and to those who asked "Where was such a book when I was coming to Canada?"

- My valued clients and all the career management and business professionals I met in person, at conferences, through their books, on teleseminars and in online communities. All helped me to become a better career practitioner and, by extension, an author.

I am indeed grateful to each of you for making this dream a reality.

Daisy Wright

FOREWORD

When I received the request to write the foreword of this second edition of "No Canadian Experience, Eh?" I felt humble and honoured. According to the universal authors' and publishers' rules, the request means that Daisy considers me a "specialist in the subject-matter" and respects my opinion. Coming from Daisy, whom I respect and admire, that means a great deal to me.

Of course, I am very familiar with Daisy's first edition, and know very well that she is a passionate and proactive optimist with profound familiarity with the subject matter. I know, as well, that Daisy writes from mind and heart with clarity and objectivity, and without naiveté. Her writing is based on her personal immigration experience, her vast professional expertise, and her unlimited, unfettered commitment to helping foreign-trained professionals compete and succeed. She also collaborates with distinguished career colleagues to ensure she provides the most current advice for those hoping to start careers in their new homeland.

When I read this latest edition, I realized that it was close to impossible to summarize its value in one or two pages. It is a challenge to offer only a few meaningful statements about its content and relevance, refer to the changes with respect to the first edition, and – first and foremost – state who should read this book and why.

This second edition of "No Canadian Experience, Eh?" came to life following the resounding success of the first. It was also prompted from the countless requests by business associates, stakeholders and friends of Daisy, including myself. She was asked to expand the book into an even more comprehensive guide for foreign-trained professionals. Daisy knew that – especially with the advances of technology – additional strategies were needed to help her readers navigate the path to success in their quest to start a professional life in Canada.

The book provides an objective analysis and a reality check of all the aspects, parameters, and reasons why immigrants face such a difficult uphill battle. Competing for employment in the Canadian marketplace is extremely challenging and Daisy knows this. Being both a fighter and an optimist, she brilliantly delivers her message and positive attitude throughout the book.

This book is not just for newcomer professionals; it is also an excellent resource for professionals who counsel others in similar situations. The book is a must-read for any professional looking for a better understanding of the challenges of competing for opportunities in today's Canadian marketplace. The book is especially intended for hard-working, self–confident and perseverant professionals committed to overcoming obstacles and adversity, and prevailing. In other words: it is a book for winners! It delivers not just a message of hope, but also a detailed, comprehensive, and flexible blueprint for success. It is anecdotic yet systematic, sometimes even funny but profound, and always positive.

Each one of us, including Daisy and myself, who came to this beloved country of ours looking for opportunities to restart our lives, knows that there is not "a right way" to professional employment integration. Most of us brought with us only hopes, dreams, and perseverance, and managed to find professional success and personal happiness Now, I invite all readers to learn from the experience of others and turn to the "The Wright Way", even if you don't have Canadian Experience, Eh?

- Dr. Yamil Alonso

Dr. Yamil H. Alonso was a councillor to the Minister of Education in his native Cuba.

He holds a Masters Degree in Mathematics from the University of Havana, and a Ph. D. in Education from the University of Potsdam, Germany.

After immigrating to Canada, he lectured for several years at York University and at the University of Toronto. He was also a business partner and Director of Education of Rowntree Montessori Schools in Brampton.

Since 2006, Dr. Alonso has been managing special projects for the Brampton Board of Trade. Through his project "Skills Without Borders", he has conducted research of labour market and employment barriers, has published extensively, has been keynote speaker and presenter in numerous professional events and, in 2009, received a Newcomer Champion Award from the Government of Ontario.

TESTIMONIALS FOR NO CANADIAN EXPERIENCE, EH?

"The book is an excellent resource tool...It covers everything from how to write a résumé, to job interviews, to Canadian workplace culture and the very real personal stories of newcomers...thank you for a well-researched and comprehensive guide."
Excerpts from a letter from Mr. Mike Colle, a former Minister of Citizenship & Immigration

"As Manager, Diversity Programs and Initiatives, who delivers diversity training at TD Bank, I am thrilled that "No Canadian Experience, Eh?" provides such in-depth insight and knowledge to employers and new talent to Canada. In a global economic environment, we need to "think outside the box" and embrace the experience and skills that our diverse talents bring to our respective organizations.

This book is an outstanding resource tool and thoroughly prepares our newcomers to take a pro-active and fresh look at addressing some of the employment barriers that they will face." ~ **Dauna Jones-Simmonds – Manager, Diversity Programs and Initiatives, TD Bank and Vice-Chair, Board of Directors for ACCES Employment**

"This is one of the best renditions of both personal experiences and professional guidance that I have read since arriving in Canada, my new country of choice. It is a must read for all immigrants to navigate the waters before and after landing as it is illustrated in a very simple and understandable manner. Thank you Daisy for your hard work and effort in putting together this guide for newcomers to Canada." ~ **Gautam Nath, Recent Immigrant and Future Citizen of Canada**

"No Canadian Experience, Eh? is a must-read for new immigrants. I wish I had this book before coming to Canada." ~ **T. Small, Legal Assistant**

"Let me congratulate you on your new book "No Canadian Experience, Eh?". I was pleasantly surprised to see so much valuable information for a segment of the population that was largely ignored in regards to the job search." ~ **K. Makra, Sentor Media, Toronto**

"My wife and I found several of your tips very easy to implement and which resulted in several positive responses in our respective job searches. I strongly believe that your tips and tactics for new immigrants to find work in Canada should reach a wider audience of new immigrants." ~ **Jay Sagar, Engineer**

"I have to express my words of gratitude for the guidance provided in Daisy's book "No Canadian Experience, eh?" This book is outstanding. It provides many valuable resources to people who plan to immigrate to Canada, and it allows newcomers to take a fresh look at the challenges they could face in immigrating, but also offers advice on how to overcome those challenges."
~ **Dr. Cheng, former University Professor in Taiwan**

"Working with Daisy and taking advantage of the useful advice and information from her book No Canadian experience, eh?, helped my wife and me to understand the Canadian job market and how to make oneself stand out when job searching. It was, therefore, not by coincidence that after sending out my résumé, I got an immediate interview and that lead to a job offer before we left the UK. I owe Daisy a lot of thanks as she made moving to Canada for my wife and me a positive experience." ~ **Carlos A., Pre-Sales Engineer & Solutions Consultant**

"This book is a very detailed and comprehensive guide offering strategies for creating a strong presence in the Canadian market for career alignment and self-promotion. I use it as a resource when advising internationally-trained professionals on how to get Canadian experience. Daisy brings her own experiences to the mix, making the book more authentic and credible." ~ **Giuseppina Russo, Multicultural Branding Executive at the Executive Training Club and NAC Financial Group**

"I am currently reviewing your book "No Canadian Experience, Eh?" as a class assignment in which I am training to become a Job Developer. Just when my frustration level was reaching fever pitch, brought on by the rigours of settling in Ontario as a newcomer to Canada, you have become a source of inspiration. I am identifying with so many of the things you have written. Thank you Daisy" ~ **M.A. Williams**

INTRODUCTION TO THE NEW EDITION

"An optimist sees an opportunity in every calamity; a pessimist sees a calamity in every opportunity." – **Winston Churchill**, statesman and leader of Britain during WWII

This book is dedicated to those new immigrants who, by sheer perseverance, made it a little easier for those of us who came behind. It is dedicated to those who continue to toil because they have seen the flicker of light at the end of the tunnel, and to the many individuals who took a chance and gave an immigrant that first taste of Canadian Experience.

Although the book, by virtue of its title, would suggest it's only for new immigrants, its contents will benefit anyone seeking to take control of their careers and move forward. It will also give the reader a greater understanding of some of the challenges new immigrants face when they arrive in Canada and, perhaps, encourage them to help these individuals navigate their way and start to make a contribution in their new country.

Every year, approximately 250,000 new immigrants - mainly from the professional and business classes - enter Canada with promises of a bright future. However, after arriving, many of them realize that their credentials are not recognized and the process for this recognition takes a long time. Many give up hope and either leave within a year of their arrival or settle into some type of a "survival job".

Those who decide to continue their search face other challenges. Even though they are coached by public or private career professionals on how to market themselves to employers, when they knock on the doors, they are met with such excuses as, *"No Canadian Experience"* or *"You're overqualified"*.

One HR Manager of a prominent Canadian company, while speaking at an anniversary celebration of ACCES Employment Services, said: *"My Company was founded by an internationally-trained individual and regularly hires internationally-trained individuals. Of 56 engineers that we hired... 36 per cent were internationally trained. I interviewed every one of those engineers and I didn't separate résumés into one pile for Canadian experience and one pile for non-Canadian experience. I looked for talent. That's what we do; we look for talent. I look for the right experience... It doesn't matter where they were educated or where they came from. Great companies look for great talent."*

For obvious reasons, the plight of new immigrants resonates very deeply with me. My husband and I were led to believe that as soon as we landed in Canada, we were going to find jobs equivalent to the ones we were leaving.

At no point during the process were we made to believe otherwise. While I found a job in my career field, though not at my level, it was not the case for my husband. As an engineering technician, he did not immediately find a job in his field but, through perseverance and a "don't quit" attitude, he found his job one year later.

As I met many new immigrants from all over the world and saw how difficult it was for them to settle down and, particularly, manoeuvre the job search maze, and as I reflected on our experiences, I vowed to write a book that would make the process somewhat easier. *"No Canadian Experience, Eh? A Career Success Guide for New Immigrants"* was born out of this desire.

One of the more poignant moments happened when I was fulfilling a speaking engagement at the Library in London, Ontario. This former teacher came to me at the end of my speech, with tears, and said:

"Daisy, thank you for this book. It helped me to get up from off my knees, wipe my tears and begin again. Right now I am exploring a teaching opportunity at Fanshawe College."

I have heard from many individuals with similar stories. It is my wish that the book will continue to encourage and give hope to its readers and serve as a guide for new immigrants as soon as they arrive in Canada, or those contemplating moving to Canada.

WELCOME TO CANADA

"To understand a country, you need to be a part of it: think of its culture, think of the opportunities and challenges it will present, and also think of your contribution, because you too can help by building a 'better you' through your immigration process." Excerpted from **Immigrant Women's Health Promotion Project – A Guide to Prospective New Immigrants to Canada**

Starting over comes with its share of apprehension and it's no different when you begin your job search in Canada. The suggestions in this book will help you prepare for this important undertaking. Since there is a high chance you will not immediately get a job at the same level or in the same field as the job you left or are leaving, be prepared to make some adjustments.

While you should look for opportunities in your field of work, you may have to do like many people who have taken jobs that do not carry the same titles or responsibilities they once had. Sometimes, gaining access to the workplace (or *getting a foot in the door*, as it is commonly referred to) becomes more important than a title.

The situation is improving as governments and businesses are waking up to the fact that internationally educated professionals (the majority of whom are visible minorities), with their diverse talents and cultures, could be Canada's competitive advantage.

At the time of writing the first edition of this book, the Government of Ontario had introduced *The Fair Access to Regulated Professions Act* that would apply to 34 regulated professions including physicians, accountants, teachers, lawyers, engineering, and others. This Act requires regulatory bodies to adopt fair and transparent registration processes, which would help newcomers find work in their fields sooner.

In March 2007, following the introduction of *The Act*, the Government of Ontario appointed the Hon. Jean Augustine, as the first Fairness Commissioner. Since then, the list of regulated professions has increased to 40 and by 2012, the office will oversee registration practices in the new Ontario College of Trades. The Act will be renamed the *Fair Access to Regulated Professions* AND COMPULSORY TRADES Act. Details can be found at **http://fairnesscommissioner.ca/en/index.php**

For the reader who might be wondering why the expression "Eh?" has been appended to the book's title, here's the reason: While speaking, a Canadian will invariably intersperse his or her conversation with "Eh?" How that came about I don't know, but it's something that's distinctly Canadian.

The "No Canadian experience" piece is a more serious matter. It's a statement attributed to those who have never previously worked in Canada. In fact, under the Terms and Conditions of Employment section of the Ontario Human Rights Code, such a statement should not be used by employers as they sometimes pose particular problems for recent immigrants. The section further states that employers should try to ensure the candidates have trade or professional qualifications without requiring Canadian experience. *(See Pg. 44* **Human Rights at Work***, a publication by Human Resources Professionals Association of Ontario in partnership with Ontario Human Rights Commission).*

The other comment new immigrants frequently hear is *"you're overqualified"*, so, be forewarned, but don't let comments like these prevent you from persevering. Mainly, it's a fear of the unknown that generate these kinds of responses. Some employers may think you are not able to perform the job, others may think you won't stay with them for long, and others might just not want to take a chance on you. **Damindra Dias**, an accounting professional who arrived from the United Kingdom more than 30 years ago, was told about her lack of Canadian experience and her over-qualification. That did not stop her from moving her career forward and eventually getting to the top of two very well-known international companies.

For Damindra, it began when her first employer took a chance and offered her an accounting clerk's position. They recognized the value she had to offer. She also credits her mentors with her success:

The two most important aspects of climbing the corporate ladder are: someone within the organization willing to take a chance on you and then willing to mentor you. Without a genuine mentor in each organization my success would have been limited.

You'll need to learn about networking. The saying "it's not who you know, but who knows what you know" takes on a different meaning when it comes to your job search. It is said that between 65 per cent and 85 per cent of job vacancies are filled through networking. By joining professional associations and volunteering your expertise, you will meet new people, hear of job opportunities, discover the hidden job market, and get an understanding of the Canadian workplace culture and expectations.

While you are networking, look for possible internship or mentoring opportunities. Career Bridge and The Mentoring Partnership, two programs that fall under TRIEC (Toronto Region Immigrant Employment Council), are agencies to research for such opportunities. The waiting lists are very long, so be prepared to pursue other job openings while you wait. The **References & Resources** section at the back of this book contains the website information for these organizations.

Another challenge some new immigrants face is understanding how their educational qualifications compare with Canada's academic standards. Similarly, many employers don't know how an external credential compares with a Canadian one. It is very important, therefore, that you get your degrees and diplomas assessed. Credential assessment services are available to help you through this process. See the section under **Credential Assessments** for additional information on this subject.

Job searching is never easy for anyone, more so for those who have left their homeland and headed for what they believe are "greener pastures". It requires a different attitude. It means you will have to eliminate the words **no**, **can't** and **won't** from your vocabulary. And it also means taking a more aggressive approach to find the job you want.

A bit of advice I would give you is that, no matter how confident you feel in yourself and your capabilities, you are going to face many situations and challenges that will initially and deeply shake your self-esteem and test your perseverance and your ability to keep moving. You are going to ask yourself many times "Why did I...? This can be quite frightening! At
this point you will have to stay away from the naysayers, negative people, and chronic complainers who will drag down your spirits instead of lifting you up.

The negative aspect of such experiences is a temporary condition. You will regain your self-esteem once the initial shock wears off, and you begin to focus and put into practice the suggestions in this book. As you associate with people who are keen to see you succeed and who will encourage you to believe in yourself, you will be equipped and ready to successfully meet the challenge of change.

SECTION I

PREPARING FOR YOUR CAREER TRANSITION

CHAPTER 1

Setting Goals, Managing Time and Managing Stress

"People with goals succeed because they know where they are going...it's as simple as that." – ***Earl Nightingale, an American Motivational Author***

Introduction to Goal Setting

One of your first tasks before you begin your job search is to set goals. Decide what you are going to do and determine how and when you are going to achieve them.

Many people believe they should set goals only when it pertains to a big investment or project, like buying a house or a car. They do not realize that goal setting is a critical element of career planning and that career planning is a very significant investment in life.

How you get to where you want to go will entail setting long- and short-term goals. At this moment, your short-term goal may be to find a place to live and get a job. Have you set a timeframe when these will happen? After you have reached those goals, what will be your next step?

Set SMART Goals

In setting your goals, you need to ensure they are SMART – **S**pecific, **M**easurable, **A**chievable, **R**ealistic and **T**imely.

SPECIFIC:	What specifically do you want to accomplish? *"By next summer I would like to teach Mathematics to high school students in Peel Region."* This is a specific statement and is much better than saying "I would like to teach."
MEASURABLE:	How will you measure or track your progress? How will you know you have succeeded? *"I will contact the HR Manager at the Peel District School Board on Wednesday of next week to arrange an informational interview."* That is a better statement than "I will call someone at the Peel District School Board to arrange an informational interview."

ACHIEVABLE:	Is the goal achievable or have you set it far out of reach? *"I will register for the next session of the Additional Qualifications (AQ) course, which starts on November 12."* This statement is much better than "One of these days, I will register for the AQ course."
REALISTIC:	Is your goal realistic or are you putting pressure on yourself? Can you really accomplish this? Do you have the necessary resources?
TIMELY:	You have to set a time within which to achieve your goal. When that is written down, it will motivate you to work towards attainment. *"By August next year, I will be ready to teach Mathematics at a high school in Peel."* This statement reminds you that you will have to do everything to reach your goal.

Time Management
By Dorothy Wright

James Mankletow and Namita Anand in their "Make Time for Success" course stated that time management is not about managing time; it is about managing priorities. No one can control time: all you can do is control how you use your time.

Time management and goal setting go hand-in-hand. They are essential skills that help keep you and your job search under control. During the job search, which is like a full-time job, a lot of emotions come into play. You may feel stressed and find that your self-confidence wanes and your fears magnified because it is taking you a long time to find a job or to settle.

Mankletow and Anand state: *"Prioritization is the key to time management. It propels you from reaction mode to action mode. Setting priorities ensures that you focus your time and energy on the important tasks and not just the task on hand."*

Taking the time to set your goals and create a plan to guide you through the job search process will reduce significantly the stress that you will encounter.

Goal Setting & Time Management Quiz

Question	Yes	No
• Do I have - in writing - a clearly defined set of goals?		
• Do I have a similar set of goals for the next six months?		
• Have I done something today to move me closer to my lifetime goals? My short-term goals?		
• Do I set priorities according to importance, not urgency?		
• Do I try to do the most important tasks during my prime time?		
• Do I force myself to make minor decisions quickly?		
• Do I force myself to take time to plan?		
• Do I keep in mind the dollar value of my time?		
• Am I really in control of my time? Are my actions determined primarily by me, not by circumstances or by other people's priorities?		
• Am I continually striving to establish habits that will make me more effective?		
• Do I make periodic use of a time log/planner to determine whether I am slipping back into unproductive routines?		

If you answered 'No' to any of the questions, review and determine what you can do to correct the deficiency. It is recommended that you take this quiz every six months.

The "Just Do It" Factor

Whatever your goals maybe...be ready to take **A.C.T.I.O.N.**

A   **ABANDON** negative attitudes and fears. You have embarked on a new journey. Embrace all that is positive and uplifting.

C   **COMMIT** to your goals. Total **COMMITMENT** is necessary for your success.

T   Set a **TIMEFRAME** within which to accomplish each goal.

I   **INVEST** (time and/or money) in yourself and your future. Do whatever it takes to get you where you want to go.

O   The **OUTCOME** rests with you. You can get considerable guidance and support from others, but **ONLY** you can make it happen.

N   Untie and eliminate all the **NOTS** that have prevented you from moving forward. Visualize the "new you". Act as if you have already attained your goal.

Goal Planning Worksheet

Area	Today's Date	Final Target Date	Date Achieved

Goal (Specific, Measurable, Achievable, Realistic, Timely)

_____
_____
_____
_____

What are the Benefits of Achieving this Goal? What will it cost to achieve this goal?

_____
_____
_____
_____
_____

Specific Action Steps for Achieving this Goal	Target Date	Date Reviewed	Date Completed
1.			
2.			
3.			
4.			

Is it worth the time, effort and money to reach this goal?   YES__ NO__

AFFIRMATIONS TO SUPPORT THIS GOAL

1. Whatever the Mind Can Conceive It Can Achieve!
2.
3.
4.

Manage Stress During Your Job Search
By Maureen McCann

Stress is defined as *"...the emotional and physical strain caused by our response to pressure from the outside world. Common stress reactions include tension, irritability, inability to concentrate, and a variety of physical symptoms that include headache and a fast heartbeat."* – eHealthMD *(http://www.ehealthmd.com/library/stress/STR_whatis.html)*

As if moving to a new country is not stressful enough, you next have to find a job. No easy task, if you have to negotiate some of the complex bureaucracies of the Canadian Federal Government assistance programs designed for newcomers and job seekers. As you learn about your new country, its society, culture, customs and potentially faster pace of life, you will likely experience significant amounts of stress.

There may be a great many things happening to you all at once. Perhaps you have just moved to a new city and left family back home to be here, or you are fleeing your home country for political or religious reasons and left everything and everyone behind to start anew. No matter what your situation, chances are that you have experienced the stress that comes along with any transition. These stressful situations impact not only you but family, friends and loved ones as well. It is important that you understand and manage these issues of stress while you look for employment.

Pretending there is no stress in your life or denying the stress you are experiencing can lead to a poor attitude, negative thoughts and frustration. Left unchecked stress can also lead to significant threats to your health.

Identify Your Stressors

In order to deal with the stress you are experiencing, it is vital that you first identify what is causing the stress and how the situation is affecting you.

Stress can be manifested in many ways. While you are in transition, it is important to keep your stress in check.

Evaluating where the stress lies will help you facilitate a change in your own behaviour to help you manage the problem areas.

Take a look at the various segments of your life and compare them to the list below. This is not an exhaustive list, so you may be able to add other areas. For now, examine these areas as they relate to your current situation:

Health

It could be said that *health is paramount*. Without health and wellness, you are unable to work, and provide for yourself and others. Take a moment to evaluate how healthy you are. Look for ways to improve your health and well-being.

Spirituality

This does not necessarily refer to religion, although it might. This section is more about self-care, taking time for you. You could enjoy yoga, walking or reading. It is about devoting time to yourself; to do the things you most enjoy that bring you comfort and pleasure. Reflect on the time you have spent caring for yourself. Much like a vehicle needs regular maintenance in order for it to operate properly; you, too, require care in order to have motivation and inspiration to get yourself moving. Take time for yourself.

Family

Many people are in the fortunate position of having loving and supportive families. Regardless of the kinds of transition you are experiencing, you may not realize that family and loved ones are watching you struggle, and are doing the best they can to support and encourage you. Sometimes, well-intentioned family members ask innocent questions that can seem quite frustrating to the job seeker. For example, loved ones may ask repeatedly about your job search:*"Have you found a job yet?" "Are you still looking?" "How's the job search going?"*

These questions can sometimes be hurtful because they are a reminder that you have not yet accomplished your goal. Next time you hear a question like that, try to clarify. You may discover that the person really means: *"Is there anything I can do to help you with your job search?"*

You may also examine the amount of time you are spending with family. Too much? Not enough?

Finance

Providing financial support to your family is perhaps one of the heaviest burdens a person carries. You want to give the best to your family but, without a job, this is not attainable. Trying to find a job that will provide you with the adequate means to support your family will produce high levels of stress, especially when you see your savings decreasing.

Personal

It is vitally important to spend time getting to know yourself. In knowing yourself, not only are you well prepared to speak about your strengths in an interview setting, you are also much more confident in your own abilities. Knowing yourself and what you want to achieve in life will serve you incredibly well during any time of transition. The more you know and understand about "how "and "why" you make decisions, the better.

Relationships

Marriage, partnership and other relationships in general are other important facets of your life. Taking the time to connect with others will give you much needed impetus as you go through changes. Continue to seek out opportunities to speak to your loved ones about the challenges you face, the steps you are taking to move forward, and the role they may play in supporting you through this change.

While your life is much more than the work you do, your career has one of the greatest impacts on the quality of your life. When you start your new job, you may find that you will spend more time at work than you do with the people you have chosen to have in your life. Take the time to monitor your health and activity in each of these areas. It will provide great insight into where you face challenges and where you can make impactful changes.

Deal with Your Stressors

You cannot change anyone but yourself.

Much as you might like to get your spouse to do the dishes more often, your child to clean their room or the hiring manager at your target company to hire you....there is absolutely no way that you can change them. The only person you can change is you.

Should you come across a situation in your life where you want someone to do something for you, and it doesn't happen, you are wise to change your own expectations of this person, rather than try to change the mind of that person.

When you come across difficulties in your transition – provided you recognize which obstacles you can move and which you need to move around – you are best served to adjust your way of thinking, your style of communication and your action plan to achieve success.

There is an old sailing expression that describes this mindset well: "*You cannot direct the wind, but you can adjust your sails.*"

What it means is that you cannot control how hard, when or where the wind will blow. Knowing that you cannot change the wind gives you the power to concentrate all of your efforts on adjusting the sail. By adjusting your sail, you will capture the wind you need to power you where you want to go. When you uncover the area where you do have control (your attitude, the way you think), then you can realize the full potential (power) to control the direction of your life, your career and all of your choices. This power to change is the greatest asset you have, and it will drive you to achieve your goals.

The Power is Within You

Managing stress can be a full-time job. When your life is in transition, the way you manage stress has a substantial impact on your effectiveness to achieve your own goals.

First, recognize that you have the power to make decisions that will directly change your circumstances. No matter how much you may feel that you are a victim of someone else's decisions, you have the power to manage your life and your stress.

How Do You See Yourself – Victim or Victor?

Make your decision now: Will you be a victim of your circumstance or a victor? You get to choose. That's right! You get to choose!

When the hiring manager chooses to hire someone other than you, you can react in different ways. You can decide that you are a victim of the choices made by the hiring manager OR, like a victor, you can put it in perspective and move on. What is the difference?

The Victim
The victim complains about the circumstance. The victim tells everyone around him how the hiring manager was wrong or discriminatory or asked the wrong questions or didn't understand what the victim could do. The victim does not recognize that it is his job to make sure the hiring manager understands what talent he has to offer. The victim blames outsiders rather than looking inward to reflect on how he might improve. The victim feels something has been done **to** him. The victim feels powerless and stops moving forward.

The Victor
The victor, when learning that the hiring manger hired someone else, chooses instead to ask "How could I have done better?" The victor looks at this as a learning opportunity. He calls the hiring manager and asks for feedback from the interview. The victor learns what he could do better next time. The victor recognizes that the hiring manager has hired the best person for that job, at that time, for that company, and that the choice was not a reflection on him. The victor recognizes that this is not an assault on his character. Instead, the victor looks for lessons to learn from this experience and applies these lessons to the next set of challenges in his job search. The victor takes these lessons, applies them across all facets of his life, and moves forward with his career.

Tips on Managing Stress

Understand what your own personal warning signs are for stress. Watch for physical, mental, emotional, spiritual, and social signs of stress, which may include:

- Headaches
- Sore muscles
- Upset stomach
- Low concentration
- Negative thoughts or cynicism
- Anger, frustration, and lashing out

If you have been feeling these symptoms of stress, look for ways to reduce the behaviour that is causing you stress. You might also consider:

- Adding exercise to your daily or weekly routines
- Finding time to relax and/or participate in activities you enjoy
- Getting more rest
- Eating well-balanced meals
- Managing your time effectively
- Seeking out the help of a professional counsellor

Because reactions to stress are so varied, it is important to take a look at your own patterns and decipher what causes you stress, how to reduce it and ways to enhance your quality of life. In controlling your stress, you will be much better prepared for the task of searching for a job.

Perseverance: The Key to Your Success

It is often said that "a quitter never wins and a winner never quits". As you start your job search and ultimately, your career, you will have to make a decision as to which one you will be – a winner or a quitter. Set aside some time to think about each of the questions below and answer them as honestly as you can:

- What is that one career goal or dream that I would like to see happen? (Dream big!)

  _____

  _____

  _____

- What negative thoughts do I need to say "good-bye" to in order to achieve my goal or dream?

  _____

  _____

  _____

- What support do I need from others to achieve my goal?

  _____

  _____

  _____

- What do I need to say to family members and friends who aren't giving me the support I need?

  _____

  _____

  _____

CHAPTER 2

Assessing Your Career/Job Search Readiness

"We all have ability. The difference is how we use it." – **Stevie Wonder, well-known musician/singer**

According to Greg Smith, author, speaker and CEO of Chart Your Course International:

> *"Pre-employment profiles are an important aspect of the hiring process for a growing number of employers. By using behavioural assessments and personality profiles, organizations can quickly know how the person will interact with their coworkers, customers and direct reports. They [assessments] provide an accurate analysis of an applicant's behaviours and attitudes, otherwise left to subjective judgment."*

Self-Assessment

Self-assessment is a very important and often overlooked step in planning a career. While assessments are not mandatory, some employers may ask you to complete one or several of these to ensure you are capable and suitable for the job or, as you will more often hear, to ensure you are a "good fit" for the organization.

In order to evaluate the suitability of work options, it is important to know who you are as a person. This involves taking a careful inventory of your current values, interests, skills, knowledge and personal qualities – your attributes. Ask yourself some questions such as: *"What do I enjoy doing?"* *"What other skills do I have that I could use if I don't get to practice my profession?"* *"What other career field(s) could I explore?"* *"Should I give self-employment a try?"*

Assessing yourself provides an effective way to measure your:

- **Personality** – your attitude, what you are passionate about, what motivates you
- **Interests** – what you enjoy doing
- **Abilities/skills** – what you are good at: writing, building, teaching, singing
- **Values** – things that are of significant importance to you, such as integrity, status and accomplishment
- **Knowledge** – what you know: your "intellectual capital"

Many of these tests give a fair idea of how you'll perform on the job, how you resolve conflicts, what you enjoy doing and what's important to you. However, as helpful as these tests are, they represent just one aspect of the assessment process. Do not rely on the results of any one assessment tool, but carefully review the results against your own self-assessment – your gut feeling – what you believe will work well for you. One important thing to remember is that an assessment is not an instant solution to your career path: it's a tool you can use to guide you.

The following is a list of common career assessment tests you may find as you conduct your job search:

- Myers Briggs Type Indicator (MBTI)
- Strong Interest Inventory (SII)
- DISC Behavioural Profile
- MAPP Assessment
- SurvivabilityPRO™
- Personality Dimensions
- Jackson Vocational Interest Survey (JVIS)
- Holland's Self-Directed Search (SDS)
- 360Reach Assessment

While I have not given a description of all the assessment tools listed above, no discussion about survival would be complete without paying tribute to one of Canada's foremost career professionals, Janis Foord Kirk, who developed the **SurvivabilityPRO™** program. It's an on-line assessment that takes about 15 minutes to complete and gives individuals a sense of their overall survivability.

It also indicates how people perceive their current skill levels in 10 different areas: technical literacy, positive attitudes, self-marketing prowess, communication, learning, information gathering, creative resourcefulness, consultative problem solving, entrepreneurial initiative, and self-management.

The 13-page report that is generated offers suggestions on ways for individuals to improve and enhance their skills, and the option for them to develop an action plan.

As stated before, tests represent part of the career planning process. Those listed here are well-known in the field and are presented to give you an indication of what's being used in the industry. They are not to be taken as specific recommendations.

Employability Skills Profile

Several years ago, the Conference Board of Canada, a not-for-profit organization that conducts research on economic trends and public policy issues, interviewed a number of employers across Canada to come up with the critical skills that employees need to have to be successful in the workplace. The **Employability Skills Profile** was developed from these interviews and lists the skills, attitudes and behaviours that an individual needs to participate in the changing world of work.

The profile is divided into three main sections:

Fundamental Skills, which include the ability to communicate, manage information, use numbers, think critically and solve problems.

Personal Management Skills, requiring individuals to demonstrate positive attitudes and behaviours, to be responsible and adaptable, be willing to continuously learn and grow, and to work safely.

Teamwork Skills, requiring individuals to work with others, and participate in projects and tasks.

A copy of the **Employability Skills Profile** can be downloaded from **www.conferenceboard.ca/education/learning-tools/pdfs/esp2000.pdf**.

Personality Traits and Transferable Skills

While going through your skills assessment, you will often hear of personality traits and transferable skills. **Personality traits** are those attributes that make up your character, such as being honest, quiet, ambitious and considerate.

Transferable skills are skills that can be carried from one job to another. For example, the ability to plan and organize is useful in a variety of jobs.

The exercise below is intended for you to identify traits and skills that you believe you have. Place a check mark against the ones that best describe you and feel free to add others.

Show the list to someone who knows you well to see how many of those qualities they identify that you have listed. Then, select your **top 5-10**. You will need to refer to them when you are ready to write your résumé.

Select 5-10 personality traits and skills that best describe you:

- ○ accommodating
- ○ adaptable
- ○ ambitious
- ○ flexible
- ○ friendly
- ○ generous
- ○ open-minded
- ○ patient
- ○ people-oriented

- articulate
- artistic
- assertive
- attentive to detail
- authentic
- brilliant
- calm
- communicative
- compassionate
- considerate
- courteous
- confident
- creative
- competitive
- convincing
- decisive
- dedicated
- demanding
- diplomatic
- discreet
- dynamic
- easy to get along with
- energetic
- enthusiastic
- ethical
- empowering
- encouraging
- fair

- genuine
- goal-oriented
- good communicator
- happy
- helpful
- insightful
- influencing
- humorous
- intuitive
- inspiring
- honest
- innovative
- joyful
- kind
- leader
- listener
- loyal
- logical
- manager
- motivator
- mentor
- morale-builder

- negotiator
- nice
- non-judgmental
- opinionated
- opportunistic
- objective

- personable/pleasant
- positive
- problem-solver
- professional
- proud
- quick learner
- quiet
- resilient
- resourceful
- respectful
- responsible
- results-oriented
- self-directed
- sensitive
- sincere
- supportive
- tactful
- team player
- thoughtful
- tolerant
- troubleshooter
- trustworthy

- understanding
- useful
- visionary
- well-rounded
- willing to try new things
- work well under pressure

Your Personal Skills Inventory (PSI)

"You have brains in your head. You have feet in your shoes. You can steer yourself in any direction you choose." – ***Dr. Seuss, prominent psychologist and author***

With the results of your assessments, whether one you have done yourself or a formal one done with a career professional, you should now have an idea of where you are in your career – what your strengths/weaknesses are, what you need to build on, which areas you need to improve and what jobs you may want to avoid.

One of the first things you should do is develop your Personal Skills Inventory (PSI) - otherwise called your "skills bank". This is an activity to get you writing down all the skills you have. It will be similar to a deck of playing cards, with each card representing one of your skills. However, when you create your résumé or talk about yourself, you will select only those skills that are appropriate for that particular situation.

In her book "Outwitting the Job Market" Chandra Prasad suggests that jobseekers should write a list of what they have to offer an employer and what their strong skills are. Set aside some time to write down everything you have done and done well. What skills did you use? What were the results?

The answers to these and other questions will help you to quantify your achievements, make your résumé stand out from the other candidates, and provide you with an inventory of your skills to help you modify your résumé in a hurry.

Consider the following questions when developing your skills inventory. Make sure to write down what you did, what skills you used and what the outcome was:

- Was there a time when you did much more than what was on your job description?
- Who are some of the people you admire and what are the qualities you admire in them? Do you have any of those qualities?
- What special problem did you solve for your company or department? How did you do it? What skills did you use?
- Did you make any suggestions that were accepted by your manager? Did any of those suggestions bring positive results for the company?
- Did you find a way to make your job more productive?
- Have you trained anyone?
- Did you help increase sales?
- Were you asked to lead or be part of a special project?
- Did you create or assume new responsibilities?

- Did you receive any rewards or special recognition? What were the circumstances?
- Did you get a promotion?
- Did you receive any compliments from customers, co-workers or vendors with whom you worked?

Identify Your Passion

By Lydia Fernandes

"Nothing great in the world has been accomplished without passion." – **Georg Wilhelm Friedrick Hagel, German philosopher**

Several years ago, I taught a co-operative education class for internationally-trained professionals. Of all the lessons and exercises I delivered over the course of the program, the unit on self-assessment was consistently the most pivotal. Why? Because every step thereafter in the course depended on the students' abilities to tie in that self-knowledge with their career marketing tools. Without that, everything else would be in vain.

Typically, the unit on self-assessment focused on identifying skills and attributes using a word bank as a guide. Students then shared specific examples of where those skills and attributes were evident in their past work history. Those examples included specific accomplishments and/or feedback they received from managers, co-workers and customers. Most students had never engaged in this type of introspective work in their country of origin. In many cases, they pursued a line of work because they were channelled in that direction by family. The need for self-assessment never really existed from a career perspective.

Being able to identify and describe your skills and attributes is important, but it is only one piece of the larger puzzle. Like knowing your duties and responsibilities in a particular job, they are fast becoming the bare minimum of self-knowledge for those who want to stay competitive in the labour market. In a world where competition is fierce and career-life satisfaction is dwindling, a higher degree of self-awareness is no longer an option. It is a necessity.

If you have completed a skills and attributes inventory in the past, I would encourage you to now dig a little deeper into self-awareness and begin exploring the inner forces that drive you. In personal branding, we commonly refer to these forces as our values and passions. Your values are your guiding principles and your passions are those things that bring you a sense of energy when you engage in them or even think about them. By uncovering them, you can make knowledgeable decisions about your career direction, feel better about the choices you make in the career-life continuum, and can communicate your value with greater certainty and enthusiasm to potential employers.

By identifying the things that ignite you, you can take your job search and career management to a whole new playing field. You can create a compelling story that will captivate employers and interviewers by weaving your passions into your résumé, cover letter, job interview and "elevator pitch". Alaina Love, co-author of "The Purpose Linked Organization: How Passionate Leaders Inspire Winning Teams and Great Results" says this about passions:

"In my former years as an HR executive, I interviewed thousands of job candidates. Individuals who were both skilled and passionate about the work and the organization consistently impressed me. Their enthusiasm was infectious, so much so that at times I felt compelled to hire individuals and then later find the right position for them. They were just too good to let slip by."

So how you can begin uncovering your passions? Here are three questions to get your thoughts flowing:

1. What is the one thing that you can talk about over and over again that puts a smile on your face every time?
2. What section in a bookstore or magazine stand would someone find you in?
3. If you started your charity, what would be your cause? Why?

By consciously taking the time to get to know yourself, you can create stronger links between yourself and the labour market, and breathe deeper meaning into the type of work you do. You will get one step closer to feeling a sense of purpose and will be able to communicate your business impact to an employer with greater relevance and confidence.

_____

Source: Business Week, September 29, 2009 – Job Hunting, Follow Your Passions

Career Assessment Benefits and Career Focus
By Susan Guarneri

The Internet is teeming with career assessments and links to articles and websites dealing with career assessments. In fact, a Google search of the term "career assessment" yields more than one million hits!

With this much information readily available, it can be extremely confusing for you to decide which career assessments to take and when. Like a deer in oncoming headlights, the default position for many is simply to "freeze" and not take any action to learn more.

Given the benefits of career assessments in defining your career focus, taking no action often means staying "stuck" in a job you hate or a job search that is going nowhere. What are some of the reasons for using career assessments to assist in the career focus process?

- **Self-insight: discovering hidden assets**
  Career assessments – sometimes referred to as career tests or self-assessments – can be effective tools to self-awareness and insight for career decision-making. When selected, administered and interpreted properly by trained professionals, they help you understand aspects about yourself that play an important role in a good career fit. These include your motivated skills and strengths, interests and passions, personality type (behavioural style), and values and goals. In addition, your personal brand, risk-taking capacity, learning style, work-environment fit and current needs can prove to be valuable information for further self-insight.

  With greater clarity about who you are, obtained through objective and subjective career assessments, you are able to use this information as a benchmark for exploring career and job possibilities. Objective assessments are formal career tests, such as the Myers-Briggs Type Indicator™. Subjective assessments are open-ended questions with no pre-set answers, such as, *"What is your ideal work setting?"*

  Career assessments have historically been predominantly self-assessments, but newer 360-degree assessments such as the 360Reach™ personal branding assessment or Profiles Checkpoint 360 Competency Feedback System™ provide even more well-rounded information via comments from others.

- **Efficiency: responding to the sense of urgency**
  To speed up the information-gathering stage prior to making a career or job decision, career assessments can provide a shortcut. With the advent of online career assessments, it is faster and easier than ever to

---

take a career test and get your results. Remember to use the services of a qualified career counsellor or career coach in this process. Many of the free and low-cost assessments on the Internet very often do not provide valid and reliable measures, and thus cannot be trusted to yield accurate results. A well-trained professional career counsellor/coach will know the difference.

The sooner you gain an understanding of the results of your career assessments, both objective and subjective, the sooner you can begin career exploration. With sound benchmarks to use as comparisons to career possibilities, you will also cut short the time needed to come to a career decision and get on with your job search for a job you will really love!

- **Self-Esteem: validating feelings and values**
  The by-products of tapping into career assessments are not only clarity and insight, but also increased self-esteem. By recognizing your own unique talents, skills and values, as well as your personal branding attributes and strengths, your self-confidence will grow; and that, in turn, will positively affect your job search. Having a career focus that includes a solid foundation of self-knowledge means you know what you are going after and can pursue it with courage and genuine sincerity.

  If you are unsure about a potential career decision, career assessments can eliminate circular thinking and confusion. Assessments such as the Career Thoughts Inventory (CTI) ™ or Career Attitudes and Strategies Inventory (CASI)™, reveal patterns of career problem-solving and decision-making which may be roadblocks. By eliminating those self-defeating behaviours, the path to action becomes do-able.

Career Focus Quiz

To be the strategic leader of your career, you must determine your direction or focus. Be proactive in looking for opportunities that align with your talents, interest and personality type, and meet your needs and values.

Without a clear focus on your career path, you may be headed nowhere. Keeping all your options open is overwhelming and time-consuming for you, the job seeker, and too ambiguous for prospective employers who fill specific job roles. As the adage goes: *"If you try to chase too many rabbits in the woods, you end up with none in the pot!"*

So is your career focus clear? For each of the 15 questions below, keep track of how many times you respond with the word 'YES'.

1. **Career Exploration Begins with YOU**
   Deep Self-Knowledge to Discover Your Career Focus

   - Can you describe your career direction clearly in one sentence?
   - Do you know the cornerstone elements that can lead to career satisfaction?
   - Are you aware of other occupations or careers that might be a good fit for you?
   - Do you know your skill sets?
   - Do you know what industries and employment sectors are best suited to you?

2. **Career Transition**
   Strategic Thinking to Thrive in a World of Change

   - Are you thinking about changing your job, career or business niche?
   - Have you compiled your marketable and transferable personal assets?
   - Do you know the future outlook for the type of position you are seeking?
   - Is your personal brand consistent with the careers/business niches you are considering?
   - Do you know how your next career change will enhance your overall career path?

3. **Self-Marketing and Career Management**
   Branded Action and Communications Attract Career Opportunities

   - Do you understand that YOU are the product you are selling and that you must effectively promote yourself?
   - Have you a clear brand identity and a self-marketing plan for communicating it?
   - Are you able to give examples of accomplishments that address your target audience?
   - Do you know how to optimize your networking efforts?
   - Are you using social media platforms, such as LinkedIn and Twitter, to enhance your job search and career management strategies?

Scoring:

If you answered "yes" to fewer than 12 questions, your career focus is hazy at best. Consider career coaching with a well-qualified professional career coach/counsellor and certified personal branding strategist as an investment that will help you to secure future dividends.

CHAPTER 3

Writing Your Résumé

A résumé is a self-marketing tool designed to get you an interview and, if it does that, it has accomplished its job.

Prepare to Write Your Résumé

The résumé, which is sometimes referred to as a CV (curriculum vitae) in some countries, may very well be the most important marketing document you prepare at the start of your job search. It is usually the first thing a potential employer sees before meeting you face-to-face. You need to spend a great deal of time creating your résumé and be prepared to modify it for each position.

Your résumé should not be a chronological record of everything you have done, but should focus on the skills and attributes the employer needs. This is the time to tell the potential employer what you did with the job descriptions you were given; the time to sell your knowledge, skills and accomplishments. What product or process did you develop? How did it impact on profitability? What cost-saving methods did you implement?

Make sure that your résumé addresses the job posting. In other words, if the position asks for someone with "proficiency in the use of spreadsheet, database, presentation and word processing applications" or "ability to work independently and provide team leadership when required" make sure the résumé includes events that clearly show your abilities in those areas. If not, your résumé may be overlooked. Other helpful information on what employers look for in a résumé can be found in the **Appendices**.

Résumé Formats

Other than the fact that the résumé should be free from grammatical and spelling errors, there are differences when it comes to length and format. The acceptable length is one to two pages, because employers don't have the time to read through several pages of information.

There are three common formats: **Chronological**, **Functional** and **Combination**. The format you choose will depend on what information you want the reader to see first.

Chronological

The chronological format, as the name suggests, begins with your current employer and goes backwards. It gives a historical timeline of your work experience and is most favoured by employers as they are able to see a clear career path. It is a useful format if you are remaining in the same profession and doing the same kind of work. It is best to use an objective or summary with this format to enable the reader to know what position you are targeting and what you have to offer. With this format, it is also easy to see if you had gaps in your employment.

Functional

The functional format features your notable skills and accomplishments gained from a number of jobs. The focus is on what you can do for the prospective employer based on what you did in your previous jobs. Your areas of expertise are highlighted much more than your job titles. This type of résumé is ideal for people changing careers, those deemed overqualified, those with a variety of skills in their field of work, stay-at-home parents, and for those whose careers have not followed a clear path. The downside is that it is difficult to find out what you did in each job, and some employers think you are hiding something from them.

Combination

This type is a combination of the chronological and functional formats. It starts with a qualification summary, an overview or a profile, and highlights your strongest skills and achievements as they relate to the job posting. It features what is commonly referred to as one's "value proposition". Because it is carefully targeted, it immediately grabs the attention of the reader.

Sections of the Résumé

Although the sections described below are relevant to your résumé, there are no rule that says your résumé has to be developed in the same order. The important thing is to have the relevant information strategically placed where the person reviewing your résumé can readily see what you are seeking, and what experience and expertise you have to offer.

- *Heading*
  This section contains your name, address, telephone number and email address. Do not add any other personal information. Some employers may even put the following at the end of a job posting: *In the spirit of the Human Rights Code, we ask that résumés not include personal data such as age, health, marital and family status.*

- *Objective or Summary*
  Many jobseekers believe they have to start their résumé with an objective. If you are remaining in the same field, if you are sure about the position you want, or if you are sure it will make an impression on the person reading the résumé, use an objective. However, if the company has more

than one position that matches your qualifications, an objective may prevent you from being considered for other available positions. It's better that you use one of the following headings: **Summary, Summary of Qualifications, Overview or Profile**.

Whichever heading you choose, this section should give the reader a quick overview of your key skills and accomplishments. You may use a series of bulleted items or a short paragraph that highlight your achievements. Because it takes a busy reader approximately 30 seconds to look through your résumé, it's important that you select your most significant achievements to grab their attention quickly.

- *Experience*
  This section lists your work history. Other titles for this area can be **Employment History, Work History, Professional Experience** or **Career Progression**. List the names and locations of your present and past employers, the dates you were employed and your job titles. In stating dates, it's sometimes preferred to use the month/year format so that the recruiter or hiring manager is not led to believe you worked the entire year when you only worked from August to December.

  It is also now customary to include a short paragraph about the company which gives the reader an idea of what product or services the company offers, how many employees and customers it has, and how the company ranks alongside its competitors, e.g., "A 1,500 bed hospital with 1,000 employees, serving one million area residents".

  Because a reader takes a very short time to review a résumé, it's important to list things that are relevant. In most cases, you won't want to go beyond 10 years of experience, unless mentioning former companies, accomplishments or job titles would make an impression on the reader. Similarly, if a long-ago position is the only experience directly related to the one you are seeking, you will need to include it.

  This section is not the place to copy and paste your job description, but should include the experiences that best illustrate your performance. Describe how you accomplished the tasks expected. Align your skills, experience, and achievements to the requirements mentioned in the job posting. You should quantify your accomplishments in terms of numbers, quantities, and results where possible. Anything that's measurable becomes very important to an employer, e.g., a statement such as "decreased expenses by 15 per cent within six months of being hired". This carries much more weight than "decreased expenses in the accounting department".

- *Education*
  Where you choose to place this section depends on a number of things. Does your degree and area of study relate to the position for which you

are applying? Did the job posting specifically ask for a diploma or degree that you have? Are you a recent graduate with little or no experience? If the job posting asked for your particular degree, make sure to place it in the top half of the first page. If you use a Qualification Summary, that would be the ideal place to mention it.

When you have made the decision about where you will place this information, list your most recent education first and omit high school if you have post-secondary education. This section is also where you would include other training programs or courses you have completed as well as your computer skills. Your heading could be a combination of **Education & Training** or **Education & Professional Development**. Make sure that you do not embellish your educational qualifications: be very specific. Do not give the impression that you have a degree or diploma if you have only completed a few courses.

Bear in mind that, while your credentials are important, the employer is first concerned with your ability to contribute to the growth and profitability of the company. If you are able to convince him or her that you will be able to make a difference, your credentials may play a lesser role. However, if you are someone in a regulated profession, like engineering or medicine, you may have to obtain additional certification before you are able to work in your field.

- *Awards & Recognition*
  Highlight any awards or recognition you have received, as long as they relate to your abilities. For example, if you received several top sales awards in your former company, you want your next employer to know about those accomplishments.

- *Membership/Volunteer Experience/Activities*
  This section is very important to your résumé from the point of view that volunteerism adds to your experience, enhances your personal and professional development, and improves your public image to the employer. If your volunteer activities show value; if you hold membership in an industry association and actively participate, you should include these on your résumé. Do not include your involvement in political, religious, and other social organizations that have no connection to the position or the company in which you are interested.

How to Deal with Employment Gaps in Your Résumé

Sometimes people take time off from work because they have to take care of a family member, to travel or to study. At other times, they didn't have a choice. They were laid off or fired and it is taking them a long time to find a job.

If you have a similar gap, you will need to find a way to account for it. Here are some tips to help you fill in the gaps on your résumé:

- Tell the truth, e.g., it took time for you to prepare, move, and settle in the country.
- List any not-for-profit roles that you may have had during the gap in the same way you would list your paid experiences – organization's name, date, title, and a summary of the job you performed. Also include any consulting or freelancing experiences.
- If you were working through a temporary/employment agency and had several assignments, list the name of the agency and group all assignments under that heading. Do not list dates if the assignment was for a short duration (two days, two weeks, etc.). Don't be afraid to include the name of the company where you did the assignment(s) and a summary of the job you performed, especially if it's a well-recognized company.
- Some gaps are better explained in your cover letter, so be prepared to state the reason(s) you were away from the workforce.
- If you took time off to study, include such information under the **Education** section of the résumé in addition to your cover letter.

Create Your Résumé

Now that you have an understanding of what's required in your résumé, you will need to know how to create it so it will describe your experiences and accomplishments.

Effective use of words is what appeals to recruiters and hiring managers. Here is a list of some common Action Verbs that you can use in developing your résumé.

Action Verbs

Accomplished	Accelerated	Achieved	Adopted
Administered	Advocated	Acquired	Advised
Analyzed	Appraised	Allocated	Approved
Articulated	Authored	Ascertained	Awarded
Brainstormed	Budgeted	Built	Changed
Communicated	Consulted	Balanced	Conveyed
Coordinated	Collaborated	Contributed	Coordinated
Created	Critiqued	Clarified	Composed
Decided	Dedicated	Challenged	Decreased
Demonstrated	Documented	Delivered	Designed
Developed	Devised	Drafted	Established
Ensured	Enhanced	Directed	Discovered
Executed	Explored	Explained	Evaluated
Furnished	Formulated	Examined	Facilitated

Fostered	Generated	Guided	Handled
Hired	Hosted	Illustrated	Informed
Influenced	Initiated	Intervened	Interviewed
Invented	Inspired	Joined	Judged
Led	Listened	Involved	Interacted
Maximized	Managed	Motivated	Moderated
Monitored	Modified	Maintained	Merged
Ordered	Operated	Negotiated	Navigated
Promoted	Prepared	Organized	Processed
Provided	Persuaded	Resolved	Reviewed
Restored	Researched	Presented	Participated
Retained	Supported	Regulated	Recorded
Streamlined	Strengthened	Standardized	Specialized
Trained	Transmitted	Scheduled	Supervised
Troubleshoot	Trusted	Trained	Taught
Transcribed	Terminated	Updated	Upgraded
Utilized	Validated	Verified	Wrote

Keywords

Keywords are very important to use when creating your résumé. These are words and phrases that are specific to your profession or industry and that employers search for when they need to find ca ndidates with specific skills. For example, someone in Human Resources (HR) may include keywords and phrases such as:

- Compensation Programs
- Job Descriptions
- Performance Appraisal
- Labour/Union Management
- Payroll and Salary Administration

A teacher may use keywords such as:

- Curriculum Development
- Special Education
- Supply Teaching
- Classroom Management

Use the space below to list keywords and phrases that relate to your profession or industry:

_____

_____

_____

The Cover Letter

Many people make the mistake of not including a cover letter with their résumé. They believe the résumé is enough to convey their qualifications and interests in the position. In fact, most employers expect you to include a customized cover letter with your résumé. It gives them an opportunity to assess your written communication skills, tells them why you are the best person to fill the position, and creates a strong first impression.

Your letter should be one page in length, ideally made up of **four** paragraphs.

- The **first** paragraph answers the "how" and "why" – how you heard about the position and why you are applying for it. If the company did not advertise, but is one that you have researched, indicate to them that you are exploring career opportunities with them.

- The **second** paragraph describes your skills, education, and experience as they relate to the position. It also shows how your experience meets the company's needs and what they can expect from you.

- The **third** paragraph specifies your achievements – how well you did what you were asked to do, what difference you made to previous employers' profitability and what makes you uniquely qualified for the job.

- The **fourth** paragraph is a "Call to Action" - letting the employer know that you are very interested in the position, what you can do for them and that you wish to meet with them to discuss the job in more detail. You can also state that you will be giving them a call.

Some job seekers state forthright that they will be following up the application with a call on a particular date. This action may appear either proactive or presumptuous, depending on the company's culture, but it has worked in many cases. However, some job applications state not to call and you need to adhere to those requests.

When writing your cover letter, remember that companies are like people. They like to know that you have taken the time to find out who they are, where they are located and who should receive your application.

You should not send a cover letter that says **To Whom It May Concern** or **Dear Sir/Madam**. It is expected that you will address the letter to someone, most likely the person who can hire you. If a name is not given in the job posting, and you have tried to obtain a name without success, you may address the letter as **Dear Human Resources Officer**, **Dear Hiring Manager**, **Dear Employer**, **(Title of Position) Search Committee**, or **Director of** (fill in appropriate department).

At the end of many job postings you will see *"While we appreciate the interest of all applicants, only those selected for an interview will be contacted."* Don't take it personally if you do not hear from them. It is normal for companies to receive hundreds of résumés in response to one job posting, and because of this, they are unable to reply to every applicant.

The Job Application

While a résumé is not considered a legal document, an employment application is a legal document. As such, honesty is crucial. Any information that's included on this form must be verifiable by the potential employer. You are, in fact, giving the company permission to check the information you have included on the form.

Online applications are quickly replacing the paper and pencil (hard copy) versions. If you are applying to a company through its website, you will most likely be asked to complete an online application. The fact that it's done online does not negate the legality of the document. It will be treated the same as the hard copy version. Before you begin the process of completing an application, make sure you have all the necessary information ready and check all your dates, names and numbers.

Below is a sample paragraph that's found on most applications.

Conditions of Employment

I hereby certify that the information provided is correct and that any false statements or deliberate omission of a material fact made by me on this application or in the recruitment or selection process may be sufficient cause for cancellation of the application and, if I have been employed, for immediate dismissal from ABC Company. I authorize ABC Company to make such inquiries respecting the above information, as is deemed necessary. I understand that I may be required to show proof of entitlement to work in Canada.

Signature: _____   Date: _____

Signing and dating the appropriate section makes it a legal document.

Résumé Quick Tips

- The role of the résumé is to get you the interview.
- An employer or recruiter spends approximately 30 seconds to review a résumé.
- It should include a list of your education, work experience, and skills as they apply to the job you are targeting.
- Make sure you modify your résumé to fit each job for which you are applying.

- Organize your information so that whatever is being asked for in the job posting is in the top half of the résumé.
- Include an "interest" or "hobby" section on your résumé only if you have interests or hobbies that you believe will fit with the corporate culture of the organization.
- Always send a cover letter with your résumé as it gives you another opportunity to include additional information or reinforce items in your résumé.

———————————————————

CHAPTER 4

Marketing Yourself

In order to succeed we must first believe that we can - **Michael Korda, English novelist and editor-in-chief**

It is not enough to have a professional résumé and cover letter. You must be prepared to market yourself effectively to employers. This activity involves more than sending out hundreds of résumés to hundreds of companies. In this Chapter, you will learn how to identify potential employers, how to access the hidden job market and how to build professional networks.

Personal Branding

In earlier years, it was easy to find a position without a résumé as people could walk into an office and talk themselves into a job. These days, as the competition for good jobs becomes fiercer, job applicants need much more than a résumé.

It is quite common to hear the term "personal branding", made famous by William Arruda, President of Reach, the global leader in personal branding. Many job seekers, realizing that the résumé alone is not enough, now work with brand specialists to help them develop their personal brands. Why? To ensure they stand out from their competitors. This concept is no different from corporations that employ advertising, marketing or branding specialists to help them stay ahead of their competitors.

Certain companies like Nike, McDonald's, Tim Horton's, Volvo and the former Enron are recognized instantly, whether in a positive or negative way. This instant recognition is known as "branding". Branding is not a new concept. Every day we make decisions, form impressions or draw conclusions based on branding. Will we purchase the more expensive "name-brand" product or should we go for the inexpensive "no-name" product?

Branding is no longer the exclusive domain of companies. As a jobseeker, you need instant brand recognition as well: something special that distinguishes you from everyone else.

Catherine Kaputa, author of "U R A Brand" said:

> *Self-branding is thinking of yourself as a 'product' in a competitive marketplace, and using strategy, tactics, image development, messaging and the other branding tools so you can maximize your most important asset, **You**.*

To distinguish yourself from others, you will need to know who you really are. What are your beliefs about yourself? Are you a confident person? How do you present yourself? Are you dressed in a professional manner? How is your verbal and non-verbal communication style? How is your tone of voice? How do you shake hands - do you extend just the tip of your fingers or do you grasp the other person's hand firmly, yet gently? Your voicemail message and email address are also part of your brand. Make sure they, too, are very professional.

Personal branding also considers other people's opinions of you. What do people consistently say about you? Are those comments negative or positive? These are some of the things that make up your brand. Once you understand what your assets are, you need to package these assets into a brand that will set you apart from your competitors.

Why You Need to Brand Yourself
By Paul Copcutt

"The great news about personal brands is that everyone already has one. The key is understanding what that brand is and communicating it to the people that need to know" - **Paul Copcutt, personal brand speaker, writer and coach**

To many new Canadians, the whole concept of personal branding can appear not just alien, but perhaps, offensive. In North America, and to a lesser extent in parts of Europe, personal branding has been around as a concept for more than 10 years. However, it was only in the last few that it has been accepted as a legitimate – and in some cases, critical – part of job searching and career management.

As a new Canadian, you have to put yourself in the mind of the average hiring manager who most likely is someone who has grown up with the branding concept, watched commercials, read advertisements, and made buying decisions based on the influence of advertising and brands. To brand yourself like a consumer product might seem false or even simple, but it makes absolute sense – particularly in a consumer-driven society such as that found in North America.

Think for a moment about brands that have had an impact on you:

- What was that brand?
- What was the situation that made you consider or interact with that brand?
- How was the experience?
- What did that experience cause you to do about that brand?
- What are the words that you associate with that brand?
- What feelings did you have?

The experience that you had with that brand might have been negative (questionable ethics, bad service, poorly made product) or positive (very reliable, great image, positive reaction from others), but that exposure has left a lasting impression with you. Now, every time you are exposed to that brand, the same words and feelings (emotions) come back.

Employers are looking for the same characteristics when they consider you for a position (read your résumé, experience your brand in an interview), and then continually as you perform the job for which you were hired (buy your brand and feel good about their decision).

This approach, very likely, is not something with which you are familiar or even comfortable. You may have grown up in a culture where to "push" yourself forward onto or into something would be seen as rude or arrogant.

Do not worry – you are not alone.

Even new Canadians coming from other consumer-driven societies have found this form of marketing themselves a very different way of doing things.

Personal branding is not about trying to be someone you are not, presenting a false image or spinning a message that is a lie. It is about being yourself, and highlighting the skills, knowledge, and strengths that make you unique. What you need to do is to showcase them in a way that feels natural to you, yet will capture the attention of the hiring manager. Authenticity in this type of marketing means ensuring that your brand is received positively by the people thinking of hiring you.

Develop Your Personal Brand Statement

Here are some steps to help you to understand and communicate your personal brand for job search success:

- Identify your strengths – either using self-assessments or former employer feedback.
- Ask a group of people who know you – friends, relatives, colleagues, managers – what their perceptions are of you.

  - What words would they use to describe you?
  - What strengths do they think you have?
  - What weaknesses do they think you have?

From that, look to identify common themes that you can highlight in career marketing documents, such as résumés and cover letters, as well as in any other form of communication, including "elevator speeches" and responses in interviews.

- Consider the role you are applying for and who else might be competing for that job. What are the elements that you have and they will have too? What is it that you offer that perhaps others will not possess? Make sure you are communicating those differences throughout your application.
- What do you know about who is receiving your application? What are the attributes they are looking for in the candidate they need to fill the vacancy?
- Can you capture, in an easy to understand phrase or few sentences, a culmination of all the above points?
  - ➢ e.g., I use my (strengths) to help (hiring manager/company) effectively (what your job role does) by (your unique differences).

Communicate Your Personal Brand

Once you have a clear brand statement, you can focus on communicating it in a way that feels genuine and comfortable to you. Identify the various ways through which you can communicate with people and choose the ones where you come across most effectively. Select those that can reach the hiring managers you need to impress.

The critical part of communicating a personal brand (apart from being clear and authentic) is to work at sending that message in a consistent way - regardless of the method or channel through which it is communicated - and to be sure it is done on a regular basis. Be persistent but do not be a pest.

Live Your Personal Brand

After you have developed your personal brand statement and communicated it, you must ensure that you deliver on what you have been saying. Every interaction that a potential hiring manager has with you must reinforce their perception of the brand that you have communicated. You cannot afford to disappoint them: if you do, they will move on to the next candidate.

Again, consider how you want to stand out from other candidate. Pick a way that reflects who you are, but is also memorable. Sometimes even leveraging your nationality or culture can be very effective. In such a multicultural country as Canada, global experience and understanding of – and respect for - other cultures is seen as a positive skill.

Also, when you finally get to interact in person, there will be a number of pre-conceived thoughts about you and your brand. You must ensure that your image, behaviour and actions reflect the brand that you have communicated and how you want to be known.

Be True to Your Brand

On occasion, what is looked for in a candidate by the employer is not something you are able to offer. Sometimes it becomes evident that your brand and their expectations are not a match. When you are very enthusiastic about getting employed and starting your career in Canada, it can be tempting to adjust your brand to suit what they are seeking. Try to resist this.

If you end up getting hired and the brand that you communicated is not actually you, that means the employer is expecting a certain person to turn up at work every day who is not really you. While that can be sustained in the short term, trying to be someone you are not every day will get tiring and ultimately frustrating, and both you and the employer will be unhappy with the situation.

Take the time to find an organization that hires you for the skills, strengths and experience that you offer and it will be more rewarding in the long term.

You are embarking on a new, exciting episode in your life and career. Personal branding is a way for you to communicate and convey the person that you are, and leverage all that is great about you.

Not only will personal branding give you a formula for success for your job search, but it is also something that you can then apply to your new job. This allows your success to continue and, ultimately, your career can be advanced. It means you remain true to who you are while being presented in a way that resonates in your new country.

Embrace who you are, celebrate your uniqueness and communicate your value.

Tips to Promote Your Personal Brand
By Daisy Wright

- Create a mindset that you are no longer an employee trying to find an employer to hire you, but a special brand that an employer wants to "buy".
- Take a fresh look at yourself to determine what is special about you: who are you and what sets you apart? Refer to the assessments recommended in the **Career Assessment** chapter of this book.
- Ask people with whom you have worked and who know you to give you feedback on what they think about you.
- Compare your findings in your assessment with the feedback from others to uncover comments that are common.
- Based on the comments, create a T-Chart, and write down your strengths on one side and your weaknesses on the other.
- Focus on your strengths to see how you can build on them.

- Evaluate your weaknesses only to the degree that it will help you become a better person, but do not spend a lot of energy on them.
- Select the characteristics that best describe who you are and package them into your own brand..."Brand Me".

A well-branded company knows its products, knows its strengths and knows how to capitalize on its strengths. Get to know "Product Me" and capitalize on your strengths.

Prepare Your Elevator Speech

One way of letting people know who you are, what field you are in, what distinguishes you from everyone else, and how an employer can benefit from your skills is to develop your "elevator speech". The term is quite common and is based on the premise that it should take you no longer than a 30-second elevator ride to introduce yourself to someone in a memorable way. In other words, an effective elevator speech is a short introduction that markets you as an individual or promotes your business.

Your elevator speech is as essential as your calling and/or business card, and résumé. You need to be able to say who you are, what you do and how you can help your next employer or your contacts. If you do not have an elevator speech, it is harder for you to communicate what you really do.

Similar to when you were building your brand, before you can convince anyone that they should really pay attention to you, you must know yourself, know exactly what you have to offer, what problems you can solve and what benefits you bring to a prospective contact or employer. Your elevator speech should answer the following questions:

1. What are my key strengths?
2. What words come to mind when I describe myself or when someone describes me?
3. What is it I am trying to let others know about me?

Your next step is to prepare an outline of your speech based on the following:

1. Who am I?
2. What do I offer?
3. What problems have I solved?
4. What are the main contributions I can make?
5. What should my contact or the employer do as a result of hearing this?

Begin by jotting down a few simple bullet points - phrases that remind you of what you really want to say.

When your notes answer all the questions above, you can finalize your elevator speech. Go back through the notes, expanding each point. Make sure the final result contains no more than 100 words. Remember, you are trying to tell your contacts or the employer something convincing and memorable about you in 30 seconds. This gives you enough information to create your calling (or business) card.

Create Your Calling Card

While it is customary for job seekers to carry around copies of their résumés during a job search, it's not always convenient to hand them out to people, particularly at networking events. That is the reason you will need calling cards. These are similar to business cards but with a summary of your skills and achievements, in addition to your contact information.

Here is a sample of a Calling Card:

JEAN CLAUDE BOUCHARD
Home: (905) 555 -0000 Cell: (905) 555-7777
jclaudebo22@gmail.com

Manage Multiple Projects ■ Achieve Results
Excel in Teams ■ Solve Critical Problems

- Ten years experience in Project Management and Policy Analysis
- Extensive experience in TQM and Productivity Improvement
- MA in Economics & Finance
- Bilingual – French/English

Identify Potential Employers

Changing countries without an employer and a job already lined up can be difficult. An excellent first step is to find employers who have successfully hired people from your country to work in Canada. These employers have already navigated through governmental administrative processes. In addition, they have experience with cross-cultural integration, enabling immigrating employees to be successful.

Three ways to find these target employers:

1. Ask colleagues, friends and neighbours for the names of the employers who hired other people from your country for employment in Canada.

2. Check online directories of people (e.g., www.pipl.com) to find the new locations of others who relocated and obtain their new employers' names.

3. Use one of the "global" lists of large companies put together by publishers like Forbes and Fortune magazines. These lists are usually online and the companies are often "multi-national". If you haven't relocated yet, you may be able to find work with them near your home and then move to your target location in Canada later.

Once you have a good list of target employers, compile a list of people you know (or people who know people you know) currently working for those employers. Ask those individuals about the work environment, benefits, salaries, co-workers and management to help determine if you'd be happy there.

Discover the Hidden Job Market

Simply stated, the hidden job market means that a vacancy exists, but it's hidden from people outside the company. Sometimes it is even hidden from people within the company. Your responsibility is to find a way to discover these hidden opportunities.

Tips on accessing the hidden job market

1. **Conduct research** that should include the news media, special publications associated with the company or industry you are interested in, company newsletters and speeches given by the company's senior management. Sometimes, it is even possible to listen to teleconference calls, such as at company quarterly meetings.
2. **Find people** who work - or once worked with - the company.
3. **Develop a short script** to use when you start making your calls.
4. Try to locate and contact the person who has authority to hire you. He or she will often know before the HR department whether or not new staff is needed.

Personal Example: **Success with the Hidden Job Market**

When I decided I wanted to teach at one of the colleges in Ontario some years ago, I sent my résumé to each college without knowing if they had vacancies. While I received a call from Sheridan College confirming that they had received my résumé, it took a follow-up telephone call from me approximately six months later to get an interview, and subsequently the position as a part-time instructor. If I had waited for the college to advertise the vacancy, someone else may have been selected. That was a hidden job opportunity.

Cold Call Your Way to a Hot Job

Sales people refer to cold calling as "dialling for dollars". From a job search perspective, we will call it "dialling for jobs", or as someone else calls it "uninvited job hunting". Regardless of what it's called, cold calling is one of the most difficult aspects of a job search and it often leaves a queasy feeling in the stomach when you have to make such a call.

So, let's face it, cold calling is frightening, frustrating and uncomfortable. Yes, it's hard work; however, if done properly, it can be very effective and might just lead to that hot job.

You must have a strategic plan before making such a call. Here are some steps to follow:

Step 1: Before picking up the phone, create a mindset that you are in sales and you are the product. Ask yourself, "What's my USA – Unique Selling Advantage?" "What's so special about me?" "Why would someone hire me?" That is, of course, your brand.

Step 2: As you would do in preparing to network, identify 20 companies in your industry or those you would want to work with, then do some preliminary research. Eliminate those you believe wouldn't be a good fit for you at this time.

Step 3: Study the remaining companies to get to know their businesses. Do not limit your research to the companies' websites, but gather information from different sources such as the media, industry associations and publications. This research should include the names of the major players in the company, including the person who could hire you.

Step 4: Prepare your script. You have studied the company, you have studied their competitors, and you are confident you know how you'll be able to help them. It's time to prepare your unique script. Avoid common scripts such as:

Hello Ms Blake, I have seven years' experience as a warehouse manager and I would like to know if you will be hiring for your new warehouse on Mississauga Road.

Such a statement makes it easy for Ms. Blake to say a curt "No" or tell you to send your résumé to HR. Instead, try something more specific:

Hello Ms Blake. While conducting research on your company, I found out you are planning to open a 100,000 square-foot warehouse on Mississauga Road, and might be looking for a warehouse manager with extensive experience in state-of-the-art Supply Chain Management & Third Party Logistics systems. For the past seven years, I have been the warehouse manager at EDF Logistics, one of a handful of companies using the B.E.S.T. Warehouse Management System.

I was instrumental in gaining management's buy-in for this system, which simplifies online reporting and inventory processes. I would be pleased to meet with you to discuss how I have been able to use this state-of-the-art system to increase efficiency and save costs.

Some hiring managers will be impressed by your initiative and tenacity, and will either arrange to meet with you or pull your résumé from the pile, if you had submitted one. Either way, it increases your chance for an interview. Go ahead. Pick up the phone and "Just Do It!"

Step 5: Assess your progress. At the end of your first week, assess yourself by asking:

- How much time did I spend on cold calling?
- Did I call new people each day?
- How long did my conversation with each person last?
- Did I follow up on leads/referrals that I received?

Your answers will tell you whether or not you need to revise your plan.

Example: How a Cold Call Turned into a Hot Job

You do not have to be a manager or have worked on major projects to employ such a strategy. An 18-year-old student saw a sign in a plaza that a brand-name pharmacy was going to open a store in her neighbourhood. She faxed her résumé as the sign stated, but also called the head office to ask for additional details.

She was given the name and contact information of the new owner, whom she called. She told him she lived within walking distance of the plaza and that she had some retail experience. Her résumé was pulled from the pile and she was one of the first people to be interviewed and hired.

This was a cold call that turned into a hot job.

CHAPTER 5

Preparing for the Interview

"Most people go into the interview thinking and worrying about how they will answer the questions, and they forget that they are there to find out about the job and the company. They forget to listen, observe, and read between the lines." – **Carole Martin, InterviewCoach.com**

Many people are afraid of interviews the way some are afraid of public speaking. However, it's a fear that you will have to face if you wish to find a job. One of the first things you should do in preparation for the interview is to research the company.

It is not uncommon for some people to walk into an interview without knowing anything about the industry, the company or its operations. They are so focused on getting a job – any job – that they don't spend the time to discover what the employer's needs are and how they can meet those needs.

Do your homework! Read as much as you can about the company before your interview. Review the company's website, request a copy of its annual report, and get to know the company's products or services. You will need this information to help you answer questions in the interview.

The second part of your preparation exercise is to get a good understanding of the interview process. Understand the types of interviews, the questions you might be asked, the questions you should ask, and how to handle inappropriate questions.

Promote Yourself at the Interview

"It is up to us to give ourselves recognition. If we wait for it to come from others, we feel resentful when it doesn't, and when it does, we may well reject it." – **Bernard Berkowitz, doctor and author**

The phrase "blow your horn" means to talk about yourself and your accomplishments. In some cultures, talking about oneself invokes images of conceit and egotism. It is especially difficult when so many people have been conditioned to believe that it is wrong to call attention to themselves. They prefer to wait for others to do it for them. Many people feel uneasy talking about themselves, and are reluctant to let others know about their personal or on-the-job successes. But as you become familiar with the interview process you will find that you will have to talk about your achievements as they relate to the job. You will have to answer the question "Tell me about yourself".

In Canada, it is quite all right to talk about your accomplishments. This is how people will know who you are, what you have done and what you are capable of doing. Taking credit for your accomplishments, in or outside the workplace, is not bragging. It's admitting to yourself and to others that you played an important role alone or as a member of the team.

Modesty has its place, but if you don't talk about yourself, you may miss out on an opportunity for a job or a promotion. If someone, especially a potential employer, asks the question "Tell me about yourself," be prepared to confidently "blow your horn" without boasting. Take credit for your accomplishments!

Types of Interviews

Employers use a variety of interview methods and techniques to select candidates. Some of the more common types are:

- The telephone interview
- The traditional interview
- The panel interview
- The group interview
- The case interview
- The behaviour-based interview
- The restaurant interview
- The informational interview

The Telephone Interview

The telephone interview has become very popular. If you have not settled in Canada yet or are applying to a position far away, you may already be aware that all your interviews will be over the phone. Many employers also use it to screen candidates; that is, you might be asked a few questions, most of which will relate to what's on your résumé. Depending on your answers and the way in which you handle yourself, you may or may not be invited to an in-person interview.

Treat a telephone interview as if it's an in-person one. Have your résumé, note pad, and a pen handy; get yourself mentally prepared, and find a quiet place where you can talk. During the call, sit up straight, concentrate, and have a pleasant smile on your face. Listeners can hear it in your voice if you are feeling flustered or tired!

As someone actively searching for a job, you should be prepared at all times. If you do receive a call and are asked to be interviewed on the spot, it is okay for you to ask to call them back in a few minutes. This gives you time to gather everything and get to a spot where you won't be disturbed.

The Traditional Interview

This is the most common of all the interviews where you will be asked questions such as: Tell me about yourself? What are your strengths and weaknesses? Why do you think you are the best person for the job? Do you have experience in this type of work? With these questions, it is very easy to give answers that you believe the interviewer wants to hear.

These short answers do not give the interviewer much opportunity to ask follow-up questions. Many hiring mistakes have been made with this type of interview, so employers are moving away from traditional interviewing and often will combined that style with what is known as behaviour-based interviews. More about this is described further in this section.

Examples of Traditional Interview Questions

- Tell me about yourself
- Why do you want to leave your current job?
- Why do you want to work here?
- Why should I hire you?
- Do you prefer working with others or alone?
- What are some of the things your supervisor did that you disliked?
- How well do you work under pressure?
- How do you organize and plan for major projects?
- Do you make your opinions known when you disagree with the views of your supervisor?
- Do you have any questions?

The Panel Interview

This type of interview means you are going to be interviewed by a number of people at the same time. This is usually an overwhelming experience as you are getting questions from different people and it's a bit harder to focus. The important point is to treat each interviewer with equal respect.

The Group Interview

This interview is a bit different from the panel interview. You may have one or more interviewers, but candidates are interviewed in groups. This is one way of determining how you measure up to each other in terms of your confidence, your ability to communicate or how comfortable you are working in a team environment. While you would want to impress the interviewer(s) it is not the time to criticize or show up any weaknesses in the other candidates.

The Case Interview

Case interviewing is becoming more prevalent these days and it's chiefly given to MBA candidates or someone engaged in consulting. The interviewer wants to know the steps you would take to solve a particular problem. He or she then observes your problem-solving skills and listens to how you answer the questions.

The Restaurant Interview

If you are ever asked to attend an interview at a restaurant, don't consider this a strange request. While the majority of interviews are done in an office, some recruiters may decide to interview you at a restaurant. This act is not meant to intimidate you or to assess your table manners. It is more to meet with you in a more relaxed and less formal atmosphere.

Although it may be a more relaxed environment for the interviewer, it might be a tensed one for you because the same interview rules apply. Treat it as if you were being interviewed in an office.

Arrive early, dress appropriately and make sure you have done your research on the company. Know the location of the restaurant, even if that means going there a day or two prior to your interview. In addition, be polite to the restaurant staff; turn off your cell phone, do not order any alcoholic drink even if invited to do so, select a reasonably priced meal, listen carefully and most of all, be prepared to answer and ask the right questions.

The Behaviour-Based Interview

This type of interview is gaining popularity with employers because it focuses on how you did the job. It is, therefore, absolutely necessary that you prepare very well for this type of interview. A behaviour-based interview is like storytelling. It will require you to recall specific experiences that demonstrate the competencies set out in the job posting. The employer will be looking for specific job-related examples of skills you used and results you accomplished.

The idea behind the behavioural interview is that your past performance can determine your future performance. If you performed well with a given task or in a given role, it is assumed you will do the same in a similar situation. Bear in mind that this type of interview also measures your ability to deal with adverse or bad situations, so it's okay to recall instances when things did not go well. The employer wants to know how you handled the situation and what lessons you learned.

You will be able to identify a behaviour-based interview when the question begins with *"Tell me a time when...", "Give me an example of...", "Describe a situation where..."*

When talking about behaviour-based interviews, you will very often hear about competencies. These are the skills, knowledge and attributes that the employer has already decided a candidate should have to be successful in the position. Some common competencies would include skills in communication, leadership, adaptability, customer service, decision-making, problem-solving, and organizing and planning.

The Rating Factor

One very important aspect of behavioural interviews is the rating factor. The employer develops a rating system to determine which candidate is best suited for the job. At the end of the interview, the interviewer assesses and scores each candidate based on the competencies and the answers the candidate provided.

Tips on Preparing for the Behaviour-Based Interview

Even if you are not in a behaviour-based interview, prepare yourself for it anyway. When you understand how this type of interview works, you stand a very good chance of doing well. Here are some guidelines in preparing for a behaviour-based interview:

- Review the job posting and identify the competencies – the knowledge, skills and that attributes – that are requested. What are the key requirements?
- Develop at least four stories for each competency.
- Reflect on your job performances and recall problems or challenges that you encountered. Develop stories around those challenges or problems. What action(s) did you take to solve the problem and what were the results? What happened as a result of your actions?
- The acronyms SAR (Situation, Action, Result) and CAR (Challenge, Action, Result) can be used as guides when answering the questions.
- This type of interview asks for specific answers, not hypothetical ones, as the interviewer is making sure that you are not making up the stories as you go along.
- Don't be surprised if some interviewers ask for proof of your stories. Who else worked on the project with you? Can they call to verify your role in the project?
- Incorporate behavioural interview techniques into your answers even if you are asked traditional interview questions and distinguish yourself from other candidates.

Examples of Behaviour-Based Questions

Communication Skills
1. Give me an example of a time when a co-worker criticized your work in front of others.
   a. How did you respond?
   b. How has that helped you to communicate with others?

2. Describe your experience in writing memos and letters.
   a. Describe the most difficult report or letter you have written

b. How did you organize the report or the letter?

Problem Solving
1. Describe a specific situation where an unexpected problem surfaced and you had to resolve it.
    a. What steps did you take to solve the problem
    b. What was the outcome?

2. Describe a method you use to solve problems
    a. Give me a specific example of a problem you encountered and how you used this method to resolve it.
    b. What was the outcome?

Team Building
1. Describe a time when you have had to lead or coordinate the efforts of a group.
    a. How did you decide which members received which duties?
    b. What were the results?

2. Describe a situation when you helped a team member with a task.
    a. Why did you feel it was important to help this individual?
    b. What was the outcome of your efforts?

Organizing & Planning
1. Describe how you deal with unexpected events on the job.
    a. Let's say a supervisor gave you a new project and you had a previous deadline to meet, what was your response?
    b. How did you handle it?

2. Give me specific examples of several projects you were working on at the same time.
    a. How did you keep track of their progress?
    b. How did they turn out?

3. Describe a specific project you planned from start to finish.
    a. What problems did you encounter?
    b. How did you handle the problems?
    c. What was the outcome?

Decision Making
1. Describe the biggest decision you have had to make.
    a. How did you arrive at your decision?
    b. What was the outcome?
    c. What would you do differently if you had to do it over again?

2. Tell me about a difficult decision you made at work.
    a. What clues did you fail to see?
    b. What could you have done differently?
    c. What did you learn?

See **Appendix II** for other common interview questions that Canadian HR managers, recruiters and hiring managers tend to ask.

Informational Interviews

> *"Worry is like a rocking chair – it gives you something to do, but it doesn't get you anywhere." – **Dorothy Galyean, inspirational author***

We have already discussed the hidden job market. Another way of meeting people and finding these "hidden opportunities" is to conduct informational interviews. In this instance, you are the one conducting the interview. Richard Bolles, author of "What Colour is Your Parachute" introduced the concept of informational interviews which allows you to get inside information on a company – what they are doing or planning to do, as well as the skills necessary to succeed in a particular job.

Your first step in conducting this type of an interview is to select a few companies and do some preliminary research. After you have settled on companies that you like, try to find someone who either works with the company or knows someone who does. Your goal during the interview is to seek information, not to ask for a job. Before you arrange the meeting (whether on the phone or in person), make sure you have your introductory script, as well as the questions you want to ask.

Below is a sample script of an informational interview:

> *"At the suggestion of Jane Brown, whom I met at the Board of Trade meeting last week, I am calling to find out if you would be willing to speak with me for approximately 15-20 minutes to give me some advice on the skills and experience necessary to succeed in a position such as yours. I have six years' experience working in _____, but would like to know what I need to do before applying for work as a_____."*

You will want to change this script depending on your area of expertise. When you make the call, if the person is too busy, you should ask when would be a convenient time to call back or if there is someone else you might be able to speak with.

When you actually meet with an individual, introduce yourself and thank him/her for taking the time to talk or meet with you. Tell them enough about yourself (interests and skills) so that he or she can offer you relevant information.

In the interview you will want to ask questions such as the following:

- What aspects of this job give you the most satisfaction?
- How did you get into this line of work?

- What skills and personal qualities are necessary to do your job well?
- How long have you worked for this organization?
- What are your major responsibilities?
- What do you perceive to be the major rewards of this job?
- What are the major frustrations in this job?
- What do you like most about this job?
- What are the most frequently recurring problems?
- Have your duties changed within the last few years? Months?
- What advice would you give someone with my qualification and experience?
- My strongest skills are_____. Do you know of any other company that could use someone with these skills?
- Are there other people you would recommend that I contact?

Tips on Responding to "Do You Have Any Questions?"

"Do you have any questions?" is asked at every interview, and is usually an indication that the interview is coming to an end. Since most people are not prepared to answer this, here are some tips:

- Never tell the interviewer that he or she has answered all your questions. Instead, use the opportunity to learn more about the position and the company, and further impress the interviewer.
- Since most interview questions will focus on your knowledge, skills and abilities (KSA), you should make sure your list includes some questions that do not relate to those areas.

Here are some sample questions. Since you wouldn't want to prolong the interview, limit your questions to three.

- You asked a lot of questions about _____. Tell me more about the specific expectations you have for the successful candidate regarding this area.
- How do you measure an employee's performance and provide feedback?
- How would you describe the company's culture and management style?
- Is there anything else I should know?
- How does the company compare with its competitors?
- Do you foresee any significant changes in the company in the near future? The next year?

How to Handle Inappropriate (or Illegal) Interview Questions

Experience is a hard teacher because she gives the test first, the lesson afterward – **Vernon Law, well-known baseball player**

In Canada it is unlawful for you to be asked about your race, age, ethnic background, religion, gender or marital status in an interview. Interviewers do not deliberately set out to ask inappropriate questions, but because many are not trained on what questions to ask and how to phrase sensitive questions, they sometimes offend candidates. Some questions can be borderline. For example, a question such as *"What language(s) do you speak, write, or read fluently?"* may appear to be inappropriate, but if it is a *bona fide* requirement of the job, it is not considered illegal or inappropriate.

If you are asked a question that you consider to be inappropriate, you have three options:

- You can answer the question
- Refuse to answer
- Use tact and diplomacy in answering

None of these options will guarantee that you will get the job. If you answer the question you may not get the job. If you refuse to answer, the interviewer may believe you are uncooperative and confrontational and you won't get the job. If you use diplomacy, you still may not get the job, but it's a good option.

For example, if you were asked the question "How old are you?" you could answer, if you don't mind being asked such a personal question; you could flatly decline to answer, or you could use diplomacy and tell the interviewer that you are between ages 16 to 64.

Murray Mann and Rose Mary Bombela-Tobias, authors of "The Complete Job Search Guide for Latinos," give some excellent advice for job seekers to **TRIUMPH** over the nightmare of dealing with inappropriate questions:

- **T**ake a step back (mentally); evaluate the question and the situation.
- **R**espond to the question directly.
- **I**dentify the intent behind the question and respond indirectly with an answer that relates to the requirements of the position.
- **U**pstage and ignore the question by redirecting the conversation.
- **M**ention the error diplomatically.
- **P**olitely refuse to answer the question.
- **H**it the road. Gracefully and professionally excuse yourself.

Excerpted from The Complete Job Search Guide for Latinos by Murray A. Mann and Rose Mary Bombela-Tobias, with their permission.

Below are examples of some inappropriate questions and their legal counterparts. They are included here for information only. For an in-depth explanation of these questions, consult with a lawyer or the Human Rights Commission.

Inappropriate Questions	Appropriate Questions
Nationality/Ethnicity	
• Are you a Canadian citizen? • What is your "native tongue"?	• Are you authorized to work in Canada? • What languages do you read, speak or write fluently?
Age Related	
• How old are you? • What's your birth date?	• Are you between the ages of 18 and 64?
Marital/Family Status	
• Are you married? • With whom do you live? • Do you plan to have a family? When? • How many kids do you have? • What are your child-care arrangements?	• Would you be willing to relocate if necessary? • Would you be willing and able to travel as needed by the job? (Maybe okay if it's asked of all applicants.) • Would you be willing and able to work overtime?
Affiliations	
• Do you belong to any clubs or social organizations?	• List any professional or trade organizations you belong to that may be considered relevant for you to perform your job.
Physical Attributes	
• How tall are you? • How much do you weigh?	• Are you able to lift a 30kg weight and carry it 100 metres, as that is part of the job requirements?
Health Related	
• Do you have any disabilities? • Have you had any illnesses or operations? If yes, list them and give dates. • Please complete the following medical history. • What was the date of your last physical examination? • How's your family's health?	• Are you able to perform the essential functions of this job? • As part of the hiring process, you will be required to undergo a medical examination after a job offer has been made.
Criminal Offences	
• Have you ever been arrested?	• Have you ever been convicted of a crime? (The crime should be related to the performance of the job)

Are You "Over-Qualified"?

Don't be surprised if you are met with "you are overqualified" when you approach an employer or an employment agency. It is as common as "no Canadian experience." However, it will become less of an issue for a number of reasons. First, employers, and by extension, their employees, are becoming aware of the skills and experiences that new immigrants bring to this country.

Secondly, as mentioned earlier, the provincial Government of Ontario has tabled legislation to combat such actions by employers. Thirdly, many new immigrants are not buying into such a concept and some have launched complaints to Human Rights Tribunals about the practice.

In an issue of the **Canadian HR Reporter,** it was reported that an environmental scientist from India was rejected for an entry-level job in his field because the company believed he was "overqualified" for the position. He successfully challenged the common practice of rejecting overqualified applicants and was offered a job.

Is Age a Deterrent to Finding a Job?

If you are over 45, it is easy for you to attribute your lack of employment success to your age, but it may not be so. First of all, no one in Canada is legally allowed to discriminate on the basis of age, and although it is known to have happened, your lack of success might have more to do with some of the same issues that other job seekers face rather than your age.

Secondly, there is such a shortage of skilled people in Canada today that employers will have no choice but to target those over 45 who are qualified, and willing and able to make a contribution. In addition to employing some of the same job search strategies mentioned throughout this book, you should read the following for additional ways to deal with the age issue if you believe it is hampering your job search success.

Bear in mind that these are suggestions based on what has worked for some people. You may or may not agree with them:

- **Focus on the skills** you are bringing to the employer and the contributions you are going to make.
- **Look for opportunities to stay up-to-date with technology**. Familiarize yourself with the Internet, email and current software programs.
- **Create a one-page résumé that de-emphasizes your title and age** (CEO, for example), and emphasizes your other experiences.

- **Target companies, non-profit organizations and professional associations** that cater to older workers or those that have been designated as "one of the best companies to work for". While not all may be "age-friendly", the majority will look on what you are bringing to the table and not on your age.
- **Visit www.en.50plus.com & www.carp.ca**, two websites for Canadian Association of Retired Persons (CARP). This association has over 400,000 members and touts itself as "Canada's association for the Fifty-Plus". While it may appear that these sites are for retirees or for people over 50, they do have a great deal of information and resources for older workers who are not yet ready for retirement.
- **Build your network** and keep connected as jobs at your levels are rarely advertised. Join professional or community associations where you will be able to demonstrate your skills.
- **Keep your options open**. Although you may be looking for full-time employment, if you are being offered temporary or part-time work, or a shorter work week, jump at the opportunity. This gives you a chance to "prove yourself".
- **Be positive and believe in yourself**. You still have knowledge, skills and abilities that will either benefit another organization or position you for self-employment or consulting.

Case Study #1: The client who thought he was too old

This client worked for a major Canadian company for 33 years. At age 54, he was given the pink slip. (The term "pink slip" means to be laid off from work or to be fired). He was laid off due to restructuring. When he met with me for career coaching, he asked if I thought he was too old, and wondered if anyone would hire him at his age. I asked him why he thought they wouldn't hire him, and what was he doing all of those 33 years.

After several coaching sessions and a résumé that focused on what he had to offer an employer, he began his search. A couple of months afterwards, I sent him an email to check on how he was doing. "I am happy as a lark," was his reply. "I am working with a [name brand] company on a contract basis and am traveling all over the country. Next week I will be interviewing with another company for a full-time job."

Two weeks later, he called to say he had gotten the full-time job, was in charge of the entire eastern region of Canada, was being paid more than he got at his previous full-time job, and he was driving a company car. "Not bad for an individual who thought he was too old." I said to him. He laughed.

Develop a Portfolio to Track Your Achievements

It's better to be prepared for an opportunity and not have one, than to have an opportunity and not be prepared. - **Whitney Young, Civil Rights pioneer**

Because of increased competition in the job market, the résumé and cover letter might not be enough to showcase your talents. As such, some job seekers are creating portfolios that contain samples of their work, which they take to the interview to "show what they know". Others have created electronic versions that they send as a link in an email. Such a portfolio is similar to a webpage. Visit **www.visualcv.com** to see examples of electronic portfolios.

You may be asking yourself why it is necessary to spend your time developing a portfolio. A portfolio distinguishes you from all the other candidates. While others will arrive at the interview with only a copy of their résumés, you will have your résumé, samples of your work, endorsement of projects you have worked on, a list of your special skills and achievements, and conferences and workshops you attended. The portfolio serves as your memory and contains evidence of what you have done.

While the portfolio, as discussed here, is primarily for you to take to the interview, it will serve as a useful tool once you are on the job. You can add all the training courses you have taken and projects you have worked on. You can also record special comments you receive from your peers, supervisor or customers. This will help you when it's time for you and your supervisor to review your performance.

To start creating your traditional portfolio, you will need a three-ring binder with dividers and plastic sleeves. The plastic sleeves will protect your documents and the dividers (with labels) will enable you to find information quickly and easily.

Some of the things you will want to include in your portfolio are:

- A copy of your résumé
- A one-page list that tells what your skills are and what you like to do
- A list of additional experiences that could not fit into your résumé
- Certificates and awards that will impress an employer
- Samples of your work*
- Evidence of your technical or computer skills
- Letters of recommendation and any other information you believe would be relevant

*Make sure you have permission to use any samples of work you have done before you decide what to include in your portfolio. In addition:

- Review the job posting to see what skills the company is looking for.
- Decide which information you will want to use that will demonstrate how you have used your various skills.
- Organize the items with the most important item first.

Send a Thank-You Letter

Having handled all potential obstacles to your job search and having had the interview, you have one very important step to take.

The interview has ended, you have thanked each member of the interview panel for their time, you shook their hands, and you are in high spirits because you believe very strongly that you have done well in the interview. Before you become complacent, there is one other step you need to take. Write a thank-you letter as soon as you get home.

Some people believe a thank-you letter gives the impression they are seeking special treatment from the interviewer. On the contrary, it's one way of standing out from among the other candidates. If the interviewer has two equally qualified candidates – you and another person – and the other person took the time to write a thank-you letter, chances are the other person will be selected.

When writing the letter, review two or three specific points discussed during the interview, reaffirm your interest in the position, state what contributions you will be able to make, and thank them again for giving you the opportunity.

Interview Checklist

In preparing for interviews, some people spend so much time focusing on it that they become flustered and may forget very important activities. An interview checklist can help to ensure that you are prepared and have everything under control.

- ✓ Examine the job posting to make sure you have the knowledge, skills and experience that are requested.
- ✓ Research the company to learn as much as you can about their operations and image.
- ✓ Revise your résumé so that it includes accomplishment statements that address the job requirements.
- ✓ Customize your cover letter with the name of the hiring manager and the mailing address of the company, and explain why you believe your skills and experience will be a good fit.

- ✓ Review both documents to make sure they are free from all spelling and grammatical errors. Ask a family member or colleague to check the documents as well. Do not rely solely on your computer's spell-checker as it will not catch all your mistakes. For instance, the software program cannot make a distinction between "effect" and "affect" or "there" and "their".

- ✓ Call ahead to get the exact location of the interview.

- ✓ Arrive at least 10 minutes early. If possible, make a trip to the location the day before your scheduled interview so you'll know how long it will take you to get there. Remember, Canadians value punctuality.

- ✓ Be courteous and respectful to everyone you meet including the receptionist or front desk personnel.

- ✓ Be prepared to engage in small talk once you're being escorted from the reception area. You may be asked if you had problems finding the location or about the weather.

- ✓ When the questions start, whether or not it's a behaviour-based interview, make sure you have stories ready to support your claims.

- ✓ Suffering from sweaty palms? Carole Martin, of Interviewcoach.com, suggests if your hands are sweaty that you try running cold water on the insides of your wrists for a few minutes. She also suggests you rub antiperspirant gel deodorant on your palms which would make them dry, soft and smelling good.

- ✓ Don't forget to send a thank-you note to the interviewer(s). Recap some of the discussions and re-state your interest in the position (if you are still interested). Even if you are not interested in the position, a note thanking them for their time says a lot about your professionalism. You will be remembered if another opportunity comes along.

CHAPTER 6

Understanding The Job Offer Process

Never bargain or job hunt from a position of weakness. Soar like an eagle, even when you are feeling like a wounded pigeon. – **George C. Fraser, Chairman and CEO, FraserNet Inc.**

Congratulations! You have reached the stage where you are negotiating the job offer. In this chapter, not only will we look at reference checking, negotiating your salary and benefit package, setting up yourself for success on the job, targeting a senior-level position and examining what employers want from their employees.

Below is an overview of how the process works and what to expect during this time. There are several things you should know. First, salary is only one part of the equation. Second, before you can actually start the job, the employer will need to conduct reference and background checks, and, depending on the job for which you are being hired, criminal record checks.

Reference and Background Checks

It is customary for employers to conduct reference and background checks on candidates they are planning to hire. This process is critical to successful hiring and is necessary to prevent dishonesty and to make sure that employers have full information on potential employees. Hiring is a costly process.

Employers should be thorough in their checks while respecting privacy legislations. Candidates should be told that such checks will be done and need to give permission for these checks to be conducted. They should also be advised that they'll be dismissed if any false information is discovered.

Reference Checks are done to confirm what's outlined in the résumé and discussed during the interview, but also to verify dates, positions, titles and responsibilities.

Background Checks are conducted to validate education and credentials, the number of years studied and professional certification obtained.

Criminal Record Checks are done to determine if there are any prior convictions.

Credit Checks are made by HR professionals only if those are a bona fide part of the job.

Media Checks are becoming more common. It's customary for some employers to conduct such a search to find out if there's any mention of the individual on the Internet or in the media.

Reference Letters are sometimes accepted, but employers will also contact references directly. This is to make sure that the person does exist, and that the candidate did not make an agreement with a friend, relative or other person to "put in a good word" on their behalf. Employers are also aware that some candidates engage the services of reference checking agencies who work on the client's behalf.

Create Your Reference Page
By Lynda Margaret Reeves

A separate page listing your references is as important as any other supporting material for your résumé. As a new person in Canada, finding people who know you – and who can clearly describe what makes you special – can be particularly difficult.

People who are willing to provide a positive reference are known as "referees". In general, three is a good number of referees to feature on your reference page. It is also an asset to have names of people from within Canada.

Who to Ask

If you have Canadian contacts that know you well and respect, you should certainly approach those people. However, if you are very new to the country, or have not arrived yet, then you will need to ask individuals in your current location.

Your referees may be current or past bosses, friends or colleagues. You should not select relatives or very close friends as a rule, since they are often viewed as being quite biased about you. Ideally, the referees you pick will be professionals you know through business, non-profit organizations, your church or professional associations.

If you are already working and looking to change your job, you may be concerned about requesting references from your workplace. This is understandable. If you believe that your current position will be at risk if your boss learns that you are actively searching, then ask others outside of the company. Always approach those whom you can trust for confidentiality.

Where to Make Good Connections

In other sections of this book, you will read about the value of volunteering your time in order to meet others and make good contacts. Once you have had a chance to demonstrate your work ethic, your positive attitude and you desire to do a great job, you will also find this an excellent way to approach others to provide references for you.

When you use Internet media to join organizations, such as groups on LinkedIn, Twitter or Facebook, you should avoid asking for references – unless you have built a particularly strong relationship with a select individual or two. For one thing, if you do not really know how credible a person is, you may have the wrong contact name in your list. Most likely, though, you will annoy online acquaintances if you ask them to speak on your behalf. On the other hand, it is quite acceptable to ask someone that has been impressed with your group involvement if they would mind putting a recommendation about you on LinkedIn*. (*You can read more about this strategy in the **Building a Network** chapter in this book.)

How to Ask

It is crucial to request permission to use the names of people in your job search or marketing material. That is not only polite, but it ensures your referees will be prepared for a call and will be pleased to talk positively about you. NEVER assume someone will be happy to provide a reference! Approach each individual separately and sincerely. Be honest and open about your plans, and let them know that you have selected them because you respect them and appreciate their support.

Once you have someone's permission for a particular job search, you need to approach them again if you decide a year or more later to apply for another position. Your referees must never be surprised to get a call asking about you.

What Information to Collect

You should create a neat, one-page document in which to list your references. Each name should be accompanied by at least one contact method and should include some, or all, of the following details:

- Person's Name: (Mr./Ms./Dr. , etc. followed by First Name Last Name)
- Title: (Manager, Business Owner, Associate, etc.)
- Place of Business: (Company/Organization Name)
- Company Address: (Full mailing address)
- Work Phone: (Business phone number, with area code plus any extension number)
- Home Phone: (Include this if they prefer being called at home)
- Email Address: (Optional, but good to provide)
- Relationship: (What this person is to you: e.g., Supervisor, Church Leader, Colleague, Employee)
- Length of Relationship: (How long have you known this person?)

When to Present Your Reference Page

Save your reference page, if possible, for presenting to prospective employers following your interview. Academic institutions (schools, universities, colleges) and government agencies are usually the exception to this. They often require submission of three references with your application.

If asked for your reference list during an interview, you can respond with something like this: *"I have a list, but would appreciate time to let my contacts know that you may be calling. May I send it to you tomorrow, please?"* (You can enclose your page with your online or hardcopy thank-you Letter the next day.) For those rare instances where you may be concerned about your current employer's reaction, it is also fine to say that you would be delighted to supply those once a job offer has been formally made.

There are several advantages to providing your reference information after the interview (or, if you prefer, following an actual job offer):

- You may realize that much of the interview was focused on topics that would be best addressed by the person you put last on your list – or someone you forgot to include. This gives you time to rearrange the list or contact the missing individual for permission to add their information.
- You will be able to give each person on your list the courtesy of a phone call. The purpose is to let them know who may be calling and for what type of role – as well as to thank them, once again, for agreeing to help.
- When you talk to each referee, offer them some idea of how the interview went and what things the interviewers seemed to highlight. That will help your referees respond well and mention things that are relevant.

Whether you have the opportunity to withhold your reference page or not, be sure to let those agreeing to be on the list know how much you appreciate their willingness to support you. This is a good way to show how you value them and it will help them to remember you in a most positive way in the future.

Salary & Benefit Negotiation

When it comes to salary negotiations, career coaches will tell you to postpone salary discussions until you have been offered the job. You may also be feeling that, as a new immigrant, you are not in a position to negotiate a job offer, but you can. A job offer is more than the salary; it includes other benefits such as professional development, employee stock sharing plans, vacation time and insurance.

Most employers are reasonable and will compensate you fairly. However, be aware that some companies have a set salary range and will not negotiate. Your responsibility is to remind the employer of your value to the organization. Here are some things to consider before accepting the offer:

- **Conduct research** to find out what the average salary and benefit package is in other companies for people in your field. Review websites such as: **www.salary.com**, **http://salary.monster.ca/**, **www.payscale.com**, **www.careerjournal.com** & **www.salaryexpert.com** to find salary information on many professions. Bear in mind that these figures are not universally applicable, but take into consideration locations (cities, regions, provinces or territories).
- **Take some time to review the offer**. Most times, employers expect that you will want some time to consider the offer before giving them an answer. Is it the going rate for people in your field and at your level? How much is the entire package worth? What other benefits are they offering? It is important to consider both salary and benefits as benefits sometimes comprise between 20–30 per cent of the full compensation package.
- **Now that you have reviewed the offer**, arrange a face-to-face meeting to negotiate.
- **Be firm with your expectations**, but be ready to compromise if it appears reasonable and if you sense they are doing their best.
- **Never use personal issues** as a way to get a higher salary. Focus on what you have to offer the employer.

Set Yourself Up for Success in Your New Job

By Sue Edwards

Congratulations! You've landed a great new job. Your excitement abounds! If you are like many people, you may also have considerable anxiety. The first weeks and months in a new job are a big adjustment and, frankly, full of challenges.

This article will help you to appreciate the behaviours that research has shown are important for setting yourself up for success in your new role with your new employer. Typically, the first 90 days in a new job is considered the "onboarding timeframe": a time when you "get on board" with your new organization and learn its unique cultural nuances, figure out your boss' style and learn your way around the organization. In my work as an Onboarding Coach, I am privileged to support a wide range of individuals in ramping up well in their new environments.

Here are some of the tips that I share with my clients:

Listen, Observe and Ask Questions

Overwhelmingly, line managers, human resources professionals, external coaches and recruiters alike say that the number one skill to focus on in the first 90-days in a new job is "listening, observing and asking questions". It seems so simple and yet it is difficult for people to accept.

Ironically, after all the time you've spent during the recruitment process being asked about your background experience and focusing on whether you "have what it takes" for the role, once you are hired, the best approach is essentially to become a learner again.

In your first few weeks, it is important for you to actively seek opportunities to meet with, listen to and observe as many different people and situations as possible. This way, when you <u>do</u> move to action or offer your opinion, it will be grounded in the reality of your new organization.

Use the early weeks effectively and soak up as much as you can about your new environment. You will be valued more for having insightful questions in the first few weeks than for offering quick answers.

Build Relationships

Building new relationships is also important for success in a new organization.

While there are various relationships that are important to build, the priority focus should be on:

- Your boss
- Your peers
- Your direct reports (if your position involves supervision of others)

These relationships are critical to establishing the foundation necessary to equip yourself for both near-term and longer-term success.

It is particularly important to gain an understanding of your manager's preferred communication style and preferences for being updated. It is also critical to walk the fine line between respecting your boss's time and being pro-active about asking for information and support.

Creating a connection with peers and direct reports at a personal level helps you to enlist their support and have ready access to information.

Respect Existing Culture

Even if you've been told you are being hired to "foster change" or to "challenge status quo", it is critical to first demonstrate interest in, and
 respect for, the prevailing culture, company history, business practices, etc. No one wants to hear "*at my old company, we did it this way*".

Showing genuine interest in what your new organization does well and giving this feedback to others is a great way of showing respect and provoking thinking about what strengths can be more powerfully leveraged. This approach uses your fresh perspective to great advantage.

No doubt you will have tremendous value to offer your organization by bringing ideas from your home county, but it is often better to first show curiosity about your new company culture and Canadian approaches to work life. Often, your new co-workers will then be more comfortable in expressing their own curiosity about the unique perspectives you bring and ideas you can share from your cultural background and work history.

Be Visible and Approach Others

Once you start in your new job, it may seem that the most important thing to do is to hunker down and get to work. However, it is equally, if not more, important that people can meet you and get to know you as a

colleague. You don't want to hide behind closed doors or in your cubicle. Be wary of eating lunch at your desk or away from others.

If others don't get to know who you are, they may make assumptions about you that are inaccurate. Canadian workplaces are generally relatively informal in that people expect to know at least a few details about one another's life outside of work. Bring in a few family photos or pictures that your children have drawn to personalize your work space and enable others to connect with you more readily.

Get Clear About Expectations

As soon as possible after you join a new organization, it is important to get clarity on:

- Expectations of you
- Expectations that you have of others (particularly your manager)

Clarifying expectations involves having a clear understanding of the mandate of the role, job description, objectives, and performance measures. You may need to be proactive to obtain the specifics. The conversations between you and your manager or supervisor should involve agreeing upon desired outcomes and behaviours.

Some helpful questions for clarifying expectations are:

- What does your manager need you to do in the short term and in the medium term?
- What does success in your new role look like to your manager?
- What do you need to accomplish in the position that hasn't been done before?
- What are your internal customers and peers expecting of you?

If your new role is responsible for supervising others, it will be very helpful for them if you clarify your own expectations, describe your leadership style, preferred modes of communication and ways you'd like to be updated.

Be Your Authentic Self

The pressure of meeting the expectations of a new role, new boss and new organization can lead some new hires to try so hard in their role that they end up "acting a part". This is particularly true for new immigrants who are often trying hard to "fit in" to the Canadian culture. This persona can be very difficult to maintain over time and can get in the way of developing strong relationships with others in your new environment.

Most Canadian organizations expect "authenticity" and integrity. Ironically, the research shows that in the Canadian culture, the leaders who are held in highest esteem are those who demonstrate the self-awareness and humility to let others know about areas of weakness or aspects of their role that they find challenging.

Some hiring managers even equate "being yourself" with having good ethics. The reverse is also true. People that are seen as behaving in ways that are inconsistent with their values or who interact with one group of employees one way and another in a different way, may be seen as inauthentic and unethical in their behaviour.

Ask For Help, Establish Support Systems

When people join a new organization, typically they leave behind the established support systems that they have been relying on for help. When you are also immigrating to a new country, this challenge is compounded exponentially. Where you might have once felt very secure in knowing who you could trust and depend upon, now you may feel like you are essentially starting from scratch.

It is crucial to develop relationships with new work colleagues to provide insight into the real workings of the company, to help get things done efficiently, and to simply be a sounding board when the going gets tough.

People who effectively leverage resources around them and are proactive about seeking help are those who are best able to maximize their impact. In the Canadian work culture, asking for help is seen as a smart strategy, not a sign of weakness.

In addition to new work colleagues, many new hires rely heavily on trusted family members or life partners, particularly for emotional support during a stressful time. Others draw on the services of an external professional coach. Some people rely on journaling and self-reflection as a means of ensuring that they optimize their own learning during this challenging time.

Make Early Decisions on Small, Quick Fixes

Some new hires put an inordinate amount of pressure on themselves to try to figure out "*what's the most dramatic improvement I can make in my first three months, so that I can demonstrate my worth?*"

> Yet, my research suggests that the best way to create early wins is to generate some relatively easy, quick fixes that provide relief for others and create tangible results. Look around for small issues that have frustrated others for some time, yet no one has gotten around to dealing with them. Eliminating a barrier that is getting in the way of direct reports' accomplishments has a resounding impact. Making early decisions on small, quick fixes allow you to demonstrate good judgment, while minimizing risk.

> By applying these tips and putting your best foot forward, I have no doubt that you will not only survive but THRIVE in your new role!

Targeting a Senior-Level Position

By Sharon Graham

If you are a senior-level job seeker, you might become discouraged when you first arrive in Canada and realize that you will be competing against Canadians that are equally qualified. Although legislation forbids discrimination, you may lose suitable job opportunities because of the lack of Canadian experience.

One strategy might be to target positions that are at a lower level, just to "get your foot in the door". Consider the ramifications carefully before jumping into a job that may not be the best fit for your capabilities. Depending on your economic situation and language skills, you may not have a choice; however, starting over in a lower position in Canada can present new challenges as you build your career. The quality of your résumé will be reduced because the job you accepted no longer matches your level and capabilities. This may be an issue for many years to come as you try to climb the corporate ladder once again and prove yourself in your area of expertise.

Transitioning to a senior-level Canadian career

- **Do not be a victim of discrimination.** One effective way to fight back is to maintain an optimistic outlook and target employers who value the education, expertise and qualifications that you have built over the years. If you must temporarily take a lower job, immediately start to pursue suitable senior positions. If you are competent at what you do, and there are appropriate job openings in the Canadian labour market, then there is no reason why you should not target those positions.

- **Update your credentials.** In Canada, many senior-level positions are regulated by the government, so if you want to get back into a specific area, work on getting your credentials, certification or equivalency as soon as possible.

- **Market yourself effectively**. Ensure you have a high-end, strategic, future-focused résumé and cover letter that promotes your value and connects with the position and industry where you are the best fit. With globalization, international expertise and multiple languages are often valued in senior roles. Feature your special skill-set as an exclusive commodity.

- **Use your high-end résumé only for senior positions.** If you are well qualified, and looking for a short stint to tide you over, don't use your senior-level résumé. Recruiters are looking for a good match, not someone who is already interested in finding a better opportunity. Any effective recruiter will discover this and disqualify you from the competition.

- **Build your professional presence and your connections**. Canadian employers want to hire professionals who are at the top in their industry. Being good at your job is not the same thing as being known as an expert. Many people are highly skilled, but only a few are sought. In order to become one of those elite few, you need to expand your network and become known as an expert. Join industry associations attend events and start to make valuable relationships with the top people in your field. You need to become visible within this "inner circle".

- **Cultivate a personal connection**. Many Canadian companies value leadership, initiative, and maturity. When you meet with senior-level people, be relaxed and confident. Speak with them as if they are peers. The key is that you must not appear controlling or arrogant as Canadians view these types of leaders with distaste. By being approachable and showing interest in those you meet, you will be viewed as equal to the senior-level job requirements.

- **Develop a strong online profile.** In Canada, most recruiters search for senior-level professionals in the online social network even before they post the job. It is in your best interest to have a presence. Once you have posted your profile, take advantage of social media sites such as LinkedIn and start to make meaningful connections with the right people who are in a position to meet with you and discuss senior-level opportunities.

- **Mention your business interactions with any North American contacts.** If you have worked with clients in North America, make sure to say that in your interviews. Formally cite evidence of your accomplishments in these areas and back them up with examples. This will help to boost the recruiter's understanding that you will be comfortable working closely with Canadians.

- **Do not ask for a lower salary than the industry standard**. Instead, sell your value. If you do not, people will either disqualify you for a senior-level position or pay you less than you are worth.

- **Consider self-employment and part-time contract work**. These are viable options for senior-level individuals immigrating to Canada. (See the section **Consider Self-employment as an Option**). These are great ways to keep current in your area of expertise and maintain a résumé that reflects your true level.

It is never too early or too late to start targeting senior-level positions in Canada. The key is not to get discouraged and to work continuously towards your goal so that you are not left behind.

What Employers Want

Most employers have three main needs that are common to their organizations. They want to know, "Can you help them make money?", "Will you help them become more productive", and "Are you going to be a good fit? " That's it! No matter what kind or level of job you are applying for, that's what it amounts to. If you cannot deliver on those three areas and other candidates can, you will not be able to compete.

In your interactions with employers, you need to show, at all times, the relevancy of your background to the employers needs. Make sure your **cover letter and resume demonstrate how your background is a good fit for the employer.** Don't go talking about apples when all they are looking for are oranges, unless the oranges will set you apart from the other candidates. In your follow up discussions with the employer, reiterate your value: "These are the challenges we discussed in our meeting and these are my strengths and experience relevant to those challenges".

Companies are like people. They want to feel special. They want to make sure that you choose them because you know who they are, how you will be able to help them grow and not only because you are "looking for a job – any job".

Employers want to know that you know your value proposition – what you have to offer; what is it that you do not only well but also naturally. Once you understand that and have proven that you can fulfill their need, then you can discuss how you can best work together.

Employers want to hire people with multiple skills who can switch gears when the need arises. They also want to know that you are flexible. Although you may be searching for a permanent full time position, don't start off with "Do you have a full-time opening?" This will limit your chances for meaningful work. Think about full time, part time and short term contract. Many part-time and contract opportunities have turned into full time jobs.

Remember, the competition is fierce. You are not only competing with other highly qualified immigrants, but with other highly qualified professionals. Your aim is to distinguish yourself from all the other candidates, and the best way to do so is to keep in mind the employer`s three main needs: Can you help them make money? Will you help them become more productive? and, are you going to be a good fit?

Understand Hard and Soft Skills

According to Nick Noorani, former publisher of The Canadian Immigrant, *"Skilled immigrants often focus on improving technical skills after coming to Canada, and they are shocked when they are told they have 'no Canadian experience'. I've realized that this albatross around immigrants' necks is actually a vague way of saying: "You lack the soft skills I am looking for in an employee."*

In the world of work, "hard skills" are technical or administrative procedures related to an organization's core business. They are the technical abilities required to do a job or perform a task, and are usually acquired through training and education programs. Examples of hard skills include machine operation, use of computers, financial procedures and sales administration. These skills are typically easy to observe, quantify, measure, and teach.

On the other hand, soft skills, (also called "interpersonal" or "people skills") are harder to observe, quantify and measure. They are required for everyday life but are also transferable to the workplace. Soft skills have to do with how people relate to each other: communicate, listen, engage in dialogue, give feedback, cooperate as a team member, solve problems, contribute in meetings and resolve conflict. Soft skills complement the technical (hard) skills, and the best news is that soft skills can be developed and sharpened through good training and practise.

As noted elsewhere in the book, most new employees fail in their jobs - not because of their technical ability but because of poor interpersonal skills. Canadian employers place a lot of emphasis on an employee's soft skills, the ability to get on with, and fit in. They believe that they can teach someone the hard skills, but it's difficult and time-consuming to teach soft skills. To test your soft skills IQ, take the quiz at **Better Soft Skills** (www.bettersoftskills.com/quiz).

SECTION II

TOOLS & TECHNIQUES TO HELP YOU TRANSITION

CHAPTER 7

Building a Professional Network

"...no matter what groups you end up participating in, remember that it's not called 'net-sit' or 'net-eat', it's called 'net-work." – **Ivan Misner, founder of Business Network International**

As timeworn as the word networking is, it is through this process that approximately 65 per cent to 85 per cent of available jobs or business opportunities are discovered. But as Ivan Misner suggests in the quote above, networking involves "work".

According to Scott Ginsberg, author of **Hello, My Name is Scott:**

> *"The term networking is the development and maintenance of mutually valuable relationships. It's not schmoozing; it's not just handing out business cards, selling, marketing or small talk. Those activities are part of networking, but unfortunately, many people's misunderstanding of the term causes them to network ineffectively."*

Scott is correct. Many people have the wrong concept about networking and because of that, they tend to irritate people they meet by networking ineffectively.

Networking opens the doors to the hidden job market and it is through this process that you can start to build your professional contacts. If you want to build your contacts through word-of-mouth, you must "work" the groups to which you belong. Make an effort to go out and meet people who can give you job leads or may know someone else who can. Networking is a two-way process, however. If you hear of leads that could benefit one of your contacts, whether or not you already have a job, pass it along.

Keep in mind that many job opportunities are routed through professional associations before they are advertised elsewhere. If someone can attest to your skills and abilities you can bet you'll be the one who gets recommended for the opening. Many people have the misconception that networking is done only when you are looking for a job. But this is not so! Continue to nurture your network after you have found a job. Keep in touch with your contacts and continue to attend networking events in case you find yourself unemployed again.

In this era of technology, the ability to network has extended online and these communities have been very effective for many people. Microsoft, the software giant, is known to recruit employees who connect to the company through its weblog (online journal) and get inside information, which places them ahead of others.

Maximize Your Networking Efforts

How often have you heard that networking is the best way to find a job, build relationships or find business opportunities? More times than you care to remember, particularly if it hasn't worked for you, right? For some of us, networking is like going to the dentist. We know it has its benefits, but we are so fearful that we either refuse to go or, when we do, we break out in a cold sweat.

According to a survey conducted by ExecuNet.com (www.execunet.com), "networking generates nearly twice as many interviews at the executive level than any other activity". If it has worked for executives, it will work for you, regardless of your job level.

You either believe in it or you don't. There are those who believe it is forced, pushy, artificial and one-sided, and does not work. Of course, many people behave just like that and give the process a bad name. Then there are those who have evidence that it works, but that it takes a lot of time to cultivate and nurture relationships, and that it is a two-way process.

Successful networking also depends on your personality. If you are an introvert you might not feel comfortable talking to people you do not know, and for you it becomes a burden. If you are an extrovert who enjoys interacting in a stimulating, fast-paced, energizing environment, then networking will be easier.

Whichever label best describes you, you don't have to be afraid and you don't need to know a lot of people for you to be successful at networking. You may have heard of the "six-degree of separation theory" that says we are only six introductions away from meeting the person or persons we want to meet. This, of course, takes a lot of effort, but if you want to get anywhere or you want to meet anyone, you have to do what it takes to get noticed. You can begin the process now by following these tips:

Tips to Get You Started on Your Network

- **Assess yourself to determine if you are an introvert or an extrovert.** Are you the one who stands in a corner of the room waiting for someone to make the first contact or are you the one who feels comfortable approaching an individual or a group?

- **Decide what type(s) of networking activities you want to pursue.** Do you want to attend an event where you meet only a few people and spend more time with those people or do you prefer to meet and speak with an individual for a few minutes, then politely excuse yourself and move on to the next person?

- **Cultivate an online identity.** This is called social networking. Familiarize yourself with groups such as LinkedIn, Twitter, Facebook,

Zoominfo.com, Yahoo 360, and a host of other social media tools. According to a former recruiter at Microsoft, "social networking is the newest fad in looking for a job, and if you are out there and are not exploiting all of these sites with information about your experiences, education, employer, interests and background, you are missing out".

While some of these sites might not appear to be business-related, if you cultivate a businesslike image, they can work for you. It has been reported that approximately 86 per cent of recruiters "Google" candidates on the Internet before they meet them, and they frequently search any or all of these sites.

- **Create and contribute to blogs that relate to your career interests**. A blog, or weblog, for those who do not know, is an online journal. Become known as an expert by writing and/or discussing trends in your field. Be mindful of what you write because, according to the website Blogger.com, "Blogs are available to a public audience like television, newspapers and radio. When you publish a blog entry, you are broadcasting this information to a potential audience of millions." To get an idea of what a blog looks like, visit mine at **www.daisywright.com**.

- **Write articles for e-zines**. If you enjoy writing, search for e-zines (electronic magazines) that match your interests and submit your articles. These will be published on the web if they fall within the editor's publishing guidelines. Again, this is another way of becoming known as an expert. One popular e-zine site is **www.ezinearticles.com**.

- **Join Toastmasters**. Becoming a member of Toastmasters is not only one of the most cost-effective ways to develop your public speaking and networking skills, but it also provides opportunities to hone your overall communication and leadership skills. Visit them at **www.toastmasters.org** to find a chapter that's close to you.

Attend Job Fairs

While attending a job fair can be an overwhelming experience because of the hustle and bustle of thousands of job seekers and a number of employers, if you are looking to get job leads, speak with employers directly, continue building your professional network, and arranging informational interviews, then attending a job fair is a MUST.

The best place to find information on current job fairs in the Greater Toronto Area is through The Toronto Employment Directory (**www.thetorontoemploymentdirectory.com/jobfairsandevents.html**). Job fairs are also announced in newspapers, on radio and on the Internet.

Here are some steps for you to follow to make your job fair experience a successful one:

1. **Be Prepared.** You need to prepare in advance. When the job fair is announced, it usually gives a list of participating companies. Select a few of those companies that you would like to pursue for potential job opportunities and do some research. This research may include the Internet, the library, calling the company to speak with someone or requesting printed material such as annual reports and brochures. The Internet is the easiest, so start with the About Us page on each site. Read up on the company to see what they are about. Next, visit their Careers or Employment Opportunities page to see what vacancies exist. Even if the types of jobs posted on the site do not match your skills, if it's a company that you would really like to work with, learn all you can about them. Prepare some questions you can ask their representatives at the job fair.

2. **Carry Résumés & Calling Cards.** Depending on the size of the job fair, make sure you have lots of professionally prepared résumés. It's recommended that you have between 25 and 40 copies. It's important that you take some business or networking cards with you to the job fair. You may be thinking that because you do not have a business there's no need to have business (or calling) cards. Looking for a job is very similar to "looking for business".

3. **Introduce Yourself to Others.** You need to be ready to tell people who you are; what you are about. Many employers conduct interviews at the fair, so make sure you are at your professional best and be ready to quickly sell your talents and experiences. The same interview rules apply at job fairs as at the company's office. Dress appropriately, monitor your body language, maintain eye contact and be courteous.

   Just in case the salary question comes up, either have a range ready to give them (your research should have given you an idea of the going rate in your field), or better, ask them for some time to think about it since your focus is more on how you could best serve them. Attend seminars and other networking events that are arranged throughout the day. These are opportunities to meet additional people and learn new skills.

4. **Follow up.** Whether or not interviews are conducted on the spot, employers will be collecting thousands of résumés and you want to make sure yours is among those they select during the first screening. Keep a list of the companies where you left your résumé and obtain a business card from at least one of the representatives. This will allow you to contact them soon afterwards, either by phone or a thank-you letter, and have them take your résumé from that huge pile for review. This act shows initiative and persistence and the employer might just

be so impressed by your proactive approach that an interview could be arranged immediately.

Volunteer in Your Community

"We make a living by what we get, but we make a life by what we give." - **Winston Churchill, statesman and leader of Britain during WWII**

The best way to understand and learn about the culture of a people is to become actively involved in the community. Volunteering is a valued tradition in Canada and, if you are having a difficult time finding a job, is one way of gaining Canadian experience. You'll be learning new skills, meeting new people, and getting an understanding of workplace culture and expectations.

Many organizations and non-profit agencies have volunteer opportunities. Visit these agencies in your community to learn more. The expertise you gain will help you develop transferable skills, raise your visibility and broaden your network. As Keith Ferrazzi, author of "Never Eat Alone" says,"...the #1 key to success is generosity. Give your talents, give your contacts and give your hard work to make others successful without ever keeping score." If you view volunteerism from this perspective, you will be on your way to being successful.

Here are some tips for finding those professional groups or associations:

- Determine what industry or professional group in which your prospective employer may be a member. For example, if you are targeting manufacturers as potential employers, there is a Canadian Manufacturing Association, which may be helpful to you.
- Source out related industry associations in the Canadian Association Directory book or local Business Directory.
- Go to the association's link online and check information on the group, membership, events, workshops, conferences or trade shows they may be hosting. Some websites even have a "job board" listing for their members.
- Attend their educational events or networking activities and take the opportunity to connect with potential employers.

These are powerful techniques to find out about your industry from a Canadian perspective, connect with potential clients, create strategic alliances and learn from colleagues. And, yes, don't forget to bring your business cards to these events. You never know what opportunities you may find!

The ABCs of Networking

As we stated before, networking opens the doors to the hidden job market. It is the number one way to find job opportunities and, with the proliferation of social media (LinkedIn, Facebook, and Twitter), it has become much more important to understand the networking process. If you've not learned this art, you may be missing out on many opportunities. Here is an alphabetical list of networking tips that will help you move your career forward.

Attend as many networking events as often as you can. It's a numbers game. The more events you attend, the more people you'll meet.

Business/Calling Cards. Have an adequate supply on hand and give them out to new contacts before you end your conversation with them.

Contact or follow-up all leads. You never know which one will produce results.

Dress appropriately for the event. If you are not sure about the dress code that's in effect, call ahead and ask.

Explain who you are and what you do in 30 seconds or less. Give people enough interesting and relevant information that they will want to contact you for details.

Find opportunities. Always be on the lookout for new opportunities. They have a way of springing up when you least expect.

Go for it! Determine beforehand how many people you would like to meet at the event and just go for it!

Help others. Networking is a two-way street, and it's in helping others that you'll be helped.

Identify a person you would like to meet and have someone you know and who knows the person make the introduction.

Join other networks or associations that meet your personal and professional needs.

Keep focused. Concentrate on the person who is speaking. It's in poor taste for your eyes to be searching the room while you are in discussion with someone.

Learn to listen. You need sharp listening skills to interpret and analyze what's being said.

Mingle. That's the whole purpose for being there. Many of us tend to stay close to the people we already know and lose out on many networking opportunities.

Never use someone's business card as a notepad (especially in front of them). If you have to, wait until the person leaves or ask for permission.

Objectives. To motivate you to action, develop a set of networking objectives or goals that tell you what direction to take.

Prepare to give. Some people think only of what they can get, but giving can be equally rewarding.

Quickly end the conversation and walk away if you encounter a rude or abusive person. You are in search of positive and uplifting experiences.

Relax. Almost everyone in the room is as nervous as you are. Take a deep breath, go over to someone and introduce yourself.

Share any information that you think will benefit your network, without asking "What's in it for me?"

Treat everyone you meet with respect. The decision-maker is not always the CEO.

Understand and appreciate peoples' differences. You will have taken the first step towards breaking down barriers.

Volunteer your services. It provides an opportunity to showcase your skills. Many people have obtained jobs or business opportunities through volunteering.

Work hard at networking. Replace the **E** in networking with an **O** and it spells 'Notworking'.

Xray. Develop your x-ray vision. This is a networking technique where you target several companies where you would like to work. Find someone who currently works for the company then begin to cultivate a relationship with that individual. If an opportunity exists in the organization, you'll be one of the first to know.

You have the skills and abilities to develop effective networking strategies. Believe in yourself!

Zealously nurture your network. Keep in touch with those who have helped you find success and remember those you've left behind.

Make Use of Online Job Search Tools
By Susan Joyce

In addition to a computer and an Internet connection, there are some basic tools that are extremely valuable for your online job search:

- **Web-based email address**: Establish one that is based in Canada. Google's Gmail is a good option as are Yahoo or Hotmail/MSN/Live accounts. Pick one and use it for your job search and communications with people.

  Note: Use a serious name for your account, like a variation on your real name (last name plus first initial, if possible). Avoid peculiar or unprofessional names that will result in your messages being viewed as probable spam and deleted without being read.

- **LinkedIn Profile**: A LinkedIn Profile is an online résumé. If you do not have an account on LinkedIn, you should set up one and become familiar with who uses it.

- **A Powerful Electronic Résumé:** Ensure you have a current résumé that highlights your work accomplishments. This is a marketing document, so be sure that it focuses on the new job you are seeking. Give it a file name that includes your full name, enabling it to be found among a recruiter's long list of electronic résumés.

- **Job Board Accounts:** Establish accounts with the appropriate job boards so that your résumé can be found by recruiters searching through résumé databases. Workopolis.com claims to be Canada's biggest job site, therefore, it is one to consider. Other job boards include: Monster.ca, CareerBuilder.ca, and ca.hotjobs.yahoo.com. Upload your résumé to those job boards, and "refresh" it every week to 10 days by making a minor change and resaving your résumé.

  Also, you may want to post your résumé on specific "niche" job boards, which are specialized job sites used by people searching for specific talent. Post your résumé in one that fits your qualifications.

- **Google Alerts:** Employers frequently search the Internet to see what is public about a job seeker, often before the job seeker is invited for an interview. You need to know what is visible about YOU online so you can address any issues that may arise. In addition, set up Google Alerts on your target job, your industry and/or profession, target employers and your target employers' competitors.

- **Google Profile**: Establish a profile with your name and photograph, so that a potential employer who searches in Google for information about you will find it easily. The information in your LinkedIn Profile Summary will work nicely in your Google Profile as well.

- **Blogs:** If you are an expert in your field who can consistently (at least once a week) write good and interesting articles about your profession or industry or other interest, start a blog. Many free "platforms" exist that allow you to write and publish your blog regularly. In Canada, many people use Blog.ca, which is very good to help establish your credibility. Blogger.com (owned by Google) and Wordpress.com are also good places.

  If you think your blog may be a long-term business or interest, you may move it to your own domain name eventually. You may also guest post on other blogs, if you can, or comment on other blogs to help build up traffic for your blog.

Leverage Social Media
By Cecile Peterkin

The competition for jobs is fierce and it is crucial now, more than ever, that job seekers diversify themselves and use all of the tools available to help them in their job search. Social media is proving to be an invaluable tool to job seekers. Those who are not using the various networking sites are missing opportunities to network and find work.

My recommendation is that job seekers network and make connections with targeted companies instead of waiting for job postings. Social media provides you with a natural platform to do just that.

Social media networking sites are not just for young people. Growing numbers of leading corporations and their human resources staff are online. Some recruiters are using social media as their first resource in looking for candidates. If you are not sure where to begin, you may want to start with Twitter and LinkedIn.

Twitter
Twitter is *micro-blogging:* a collection of ongoing conversations in which you can participate at any time. Twitter is good for sharing useful information you might find on the Web, the latest news, your most recent (or most popular) blog post, and your thoughts about a specific industry. View Twitter as your own "news wire" and your followers as your friends and readers.

For beginners, Twitter can be an overwhelming experience where 140-character "tweets" – or mini-messages – appear every second of every day. However, you can build a following and follow people with Twitter accounts of interest to you. TweetDeck is a tool which enables you to organize Tweets.

On Twitter, you have to be active. You must work at building a following and participating in conversations. The more you engage, the more contacts and relationships you will have - and that is what can help you land your next job.

By creating a Twitter bio that reflects your career interests, you are letting other Twitter users know what areas you are looking to share or gather information and have conversations about. You can connect with people in your areas of interest, such as finance, non-profit organizations, human resources or technology.

LinkedIn

LinkedIn is an international business networking site where you can find former colleagues, connect with industry experts and search job postings. Already, there are over 75 million registered users, including executives from Fortune 500 companies. Bell, TD Bank, Loblaw and Canwest are all on LinkedIn and are using it to recruit new staff.

Another advantage to LinkedIn is that your contacts can introduce you to their contacts. There is no better way to meet potential employers than being recommended by a mutual contact. On LinkedIn, you can post your résumé for free, making it accessible to the hundreds of recruiters who are there looking for people like you. Here are some tips to get you started:

- Create your LinkedIn Profile to provide a clear picture of who you are, how you have succeeded in the past, and what you want to do. LinkedIn is enormously popular with recruiters, and is viewed as much more effective for job search than the job boards.
- Get LinkedIn recommendations from people who are familiar with your work.
- Establish connections with those people working at potential employers who could help you network towards a job, in addition to other people you know in Canada.
- List all the languages you speak and write in your LinkedIn Profile. Being multilingual is a competitive advantage, particularly in large, multinational organizations.
- Add your job search email address to your Profile summary so it will be easy for employers to reach you.
- Include the accomplishments from your résumé in your Profile's summary, too.
- Make your personal headline a summary of your target job, without indicating your location.
- Join appropriate LinkedIn Groups and participate (carefully!) in group discussions. This is a good way to demonstrate your knowledge, language skills and interests.
- Continue to keep your LinkedIn Profile up to date, add connections and recommendations, and stay active in the groups that are most important and relevant to your work.

Through these and other social media sites, you can actively search for a job and build relationships with industry colleagues. You will hear of networking events where you can meet your online contacts face-to-face.

If you are using social media for job searching, remember your photo is most often the first impression that people will get from you. It is important that your photo is clear, appropriate, and professional. Social media is about being open and sharing, not hiding behind icons or blank images.

Equally important to keep in mind is that whatever you post on social media sites can be viewed by anyone. It's not unusual for potential employers to look for your online presence before hiring. Be very professional in everything you do on these social networking sites and don't post anything that you wouldn't want a prospective employer to read.

Social media is the modern means of networking. In any job search, you are in the business of promoting yourself. Learning to ride the wave of social media through sites such as Twitter and LinkedIn will make you more marketable, expand your networks, and help to improve your opportunity to find and land that ideal job.

In summary, here are some tips to help you utilize social media in your job search:

- Whatever you post on social media sites can be viewed by anyone, so make yourself marketable and engaging.
- For your online profile, it is important that your photo is clear, appropriate and professional, not hiding behind icons or blank images.
- By creating a Twitter bio that reflects your career interests, you are letting other Twitter users know what areas you are looking to share information and have conversations about.
- On Twitter, the more you engage, the more contacts and relationships you build and that is what will help you land your next job.
- By re-tweeting posts (repeating a Tweet) on Twitter, you can garner the attention of industry contacts you want to build and network.
- You can also post your résumé for free on LinkedIn, making it accessible to the hundreds of recruiters who are there looking for people like you.
- On LinkedIn, your contacts can introduce you to their contacts, and there is no better way to meet potential employers than being recommended by a mutual contact.
- You can ask industry experts questions and garner insightful feedback in regards to your job search through Twitter and LinkedIn.
- A tweet or a message from a LinkedIn colleague may alert you of a networking event, where you can meet your online contacts face-to-face, and help to improve your opportunity to find and land your dream job.
- Actively use social media, be it tweeting or posting comments to industry discussion boards, in order to get comfortable with the

medium. Your ease in using social media will be evident to job recruiters and add to your online reputation.

- Don't spend a lot of your time applying for jobs online at many of the more popular job sites. Few jobs are actually filled that way. Having your résumé posted on those sites, however, makes you visible to recruiters. Being found by a recruiter is usually more effective than applying for a job.
- Do keep track of the job market - particularly jobs posted by your target employers - by checking their websites' career pages. *Job aggregators* are other places where you can keep current on the job market. Indeed.ca collects (i.e., *aggregates)* jobs from many sources, including large job boards, newspaper classifieds, association websites and individual employer websites. Canada.LinkUp.com gathers jobs only from employer websites.

Note: (Maureen McCann also contributed to these LinkedIn tips)

Online Presence Checklist
By Tanya Sinclair

As mentioned several times in this book, many potential employers now research candidates online using Google or other internet search engines. This is to learn more about their applicants and to weed out unsuitable job candidates. As a job applicant, it's important to ensure that all your online communications are professional and properly present the image you would want potential employers to see. Make sure you don't get any unpleasant surprises during the hiring process should there be something questionable about you online.

Email, instant messages, blogs, profiles and the content and photos you post on social media networking sites like MySpace, Facebook and Twitter can tell an employer a lot about you.

Here's a quick list of what you should do:

- ✓ Check periodically to ensure that all the information in your social media sites are professional.
- ✓ Look at your online pictures and photos to ensure they are presenting positive image.
- ✓ Google yourself to see what other people or organizations may have posted about you.
- ✓ Ensure your email address and instant messenger screen name(s) are professional. Hot_2_trot@hotmail.com, for example, is inappropriate and may turn off potential employers.
- ✓ Avoid mixing business with pleasure. Create a dedicated email address and screen name that you use just for job searching.

✓ Make sure that your email messages include a signature at the bottom of the message with your phone number where employers may contact you.

Make Your Résumé "Cyber-Safe"
By Susan Joyce

Modify the content of your résumé to make it "cyber-safe"! Take control and create your own privacy protection without depending on an online jobsite to do it for you.

This way, you will help to protect your identity and your current job, if you have one. As your résumé circulates in cyberspace over time, your "cyber-safe résumé" will protect your identity and, possibly, your future employment many years from now.

However, there is a trade-off – privacy for security. As you seek to protect your online identity, you will make it more difficult for recruiters to reach you, at least initially, because of the limited contact information that you post online. It's your choice.

Minimal contact information makes it harder for your identity to be stolen or for your current employer to discover that you are job searching. To do this, you should:

- Remove your standard "contact information":
    o Your home and/or work address(es)
    o Your home and/or work phone number(s)
    o Your business email address (This absolutely must NOT appear!)
    o Your personal email address if it is associated with your detailed profile (as in AOL, etc.)

- Replace the standard contact information with:
    o Your personal cell phone number, assuming that it is unlisted (ensure it rolls over to a personal voicemail account if you don't answer).
    o Your personal email address that is unconnected with either your home or your work, like one of the web-based email addresses such as Hotmail.com, Gmail, or MSN.

Modify your employment history, particularly for your current job, to minimize the possibility that your existing employer will find your résumé and think you are planning to leave.

- Remove your current employer's name; replacing it with an *accurate but generic*, description such as:
    o "Nuts n' Bolts Distributors, Inc." can be "small construction supplies distributor"

- o "IBM" becomes "multinational information technology company"

- If your job title is unique, replace your title with an *accurate but generic*" title:
  - o "London Gadget Marketing Director" becomes "UK marketing manager of gadget-class products"

You increase the probability of a confidential job search by being very selective about where you post your résumé.

One primary source of revenue for many job sites is that generated by selling employers access to résumé databases. For some job sites, anyone who can afford the cost gains access. So, your complete work history, education and contact information are available to anyone who can pay the access fee – employers and recruiters, hopefully – but also sales people, scammers, identity thieves, etc.

You should also be aware that there are bogus job sites collecting information from job seekers. See the job search scam articles at **www.job-hunt.org** for more information.

Protect Your Privacy Online

What are the risks of not protecting your privacy online?

- If you have a job and your employer finds your résumé online, you may be looked upon unfavourably.

  Employers often view job-seeking employees as "disloyal" – potential risks for taking clients and/or confidential information to a competitor. In the US, firing you for job hunting is perfectly legal. While that is not the case in Canada, being found on a job-search site may have a negative effect on your relationship with your current employer.

  This problem has a dangerous corollary: after you've landed your new job, your new employer may find your old résumé online and become very concerned about your intent to stay for any length of time.

- Someone could steal your identity.
- You may be buried with "spam" (bulk, unsolicited, commercial e-mail) as well as direct marketing to your home or business.
- Your résumé, with completed contact and employment information provides vital information for others to find you.
- Unethical recruiters may ruin job opportunities for you. Without your knowledge or permission, recruiters may "shop" your résumé around to employers. Why is this not good?

- Because you and your experience may be misrepresented, giving an employer a bad impression of you.
- If you have sent that employer a résumé yourself, you could lose out on a job because the employer may not want to hassle with the recruiter over a commission payment that may, or may not, be due to the recruiter.
- You will be more expensive to hire than someone else with the same salary, because of the commission due to the recruiter.
- Your résumé may be so widely distributed that it becomes "junk mail", reducing your market value.

Note: Most recruiters are very ethical. A good recruiter who knows you and works with you *can* be a big help. In fact, for some fields and at very high job levels, recruiters are the source of job opportunities.

Use these pointers with caution as they assume that your existing employer and culture will not penalize you for this activity. If anything written here will cause you harm in your own country, modify or ignore the advice as you deem appropriate. In some countries, people have lost their jobs when their employers found their résumés on a job board, so always take care.

CHAPTER 8

Exploring Other Job / Career Options

The Role of Career Service Providers

You will learn very soon that it is impossible to go it alone. You are going to need allies – people who can help you navigate your way through the job search process.

One of the great characteristics about Canada is that the various levels of government offer a variety of social services to its people. There are hundreds of non-profit agencies that provide job search assistance to new immigrants as well as to those who are unemployed. I encourage you to take advantage of these services because they are provided free-of-cost to you.

That said, it would be remiss of me if I do not mention private career practitioners, such as myself, who offer similar services. Private practitioners, as a rule, are not funded by governments, so clients pay out of their own pockets. One main advantage of this is the one-on-one personal attention that clients receive at an accelerated pace. We cover the critical areas that will get you "up and running" in a shorter timeframe, while offering continued support over a stipulated period. We decide how many people we can adequately work with, and are not hampered by a heavy caseload.

One note of caution: Before you enter into any agreement with private practitioners, make sure to do your research. Find out who we are and what we offer, and don't be afraid to ask for references. Some people may promise to find you a job, and if your research proves that they can, by all means, engage their services, because that's your goal. However, the majority (non-profit and private) will provide guidance and prepare you to the point of getting interviews, but after that, everything is in your hands. It is up to you to convince the interviewer that you are the best candidate for the job.

Consider Internships, Co-ops & Mentoring Programs

Participating in internships is another way for a new immigrant to enter the Canadian labour market. Such an arrangement benefits both the individual and the organization as it acts as a bridge between industry and individuals. Internships present a low-risk, cost-effective way for Canadian organizations to tap into the skilled immigrant talent pool and for the skilled immigrant to gain Canadian experience.

Bridging Programs
Career Bridge (**www.careerbridge.ca**), designed to assist people trained outside of Canada with gaining "Canadian experience", is an innovative

initiative that places newcomers in a four-month internship program. Host organizations commit to provide relevant work experience for individuals, and many who have completed the program have gained full-time employment - in many cases, with the same organization. All applicants are pre-screened for language skills, educational qualifications and international experience prior to being placed.

Even if you are accepted in the program, there is no guarantee that you will get an internship position. Internship openings are posted on the company's website. If you determine that the position matches your qualification and experience you would submit an online application. The company will then contact you if they feel you meet their requirements. The downside to the program is that there are far too many people and too few spaces.

Another program, which is similar to Career Bridge's Internship Program, is a Co-op Work Placement program offered by the Dufferin-Peel Catholic School Board (**www.dpcdsb.org/coopcentre**). It's an 11-week Co-op Work Placement program which provides both an in-class component and a field placement in a company or sector the participant has chosen.

This program has many advantages. It's an opportunity to gain Canadian work experience, network with other people; find people who will act as a reference, and, possibly, find paid employment.

These programs are designed to help people in different professions gain jobs that are commensurate with their experience and qualification. However, because of the high demand of job-seekers and the limited number of jobs available, these programs are considered by some people to be ineffective in meeting the needs of internationally-educated professionals.

The Mentoring Partnership

One of the most successful and innovative programs to be implemented in the Greater Toronto Area (GTA) is The Mentoring Partnership. Offered under the umbrella of the Toronto Region Immigrant Employment Council (TRIEC), The Mentoring Partnership offers occupation-specific mentoring to skilled immigrants by matching them with established professionals. To participate in the program, immigrants must possess the education, experience and language skills needed to excel in the workforce.

The Mentoring Partnership provides learning opportunities for both mentee and mentor. Mentors pass on their real-life experiences and knowledge and give assistance to the new immigrant in making connections. The mentee enriches the life of the mentor by passing on valuable educational and cultural lessons.

Consider Self-Employment as an Option
By Ingrid Norrish

It is well documented that immigrants have an excellent track record of creating successful businesses in Canada, and while entrepreneurship is not for everyone, it's worth exploring.

Many companies offer "contract" or "consulting" job opportunities and, for some of them, you may have to set-up your own business to invoice the company to pay for your services. This is often the simplest way to become an entrepreneur.

If you have a special expertise in a specific area, starting a business may be a good way to get Canadian experience in your particular industry: discover how others operate and price their goods and services, and get your foot in the door. It can become valued Canadian experience to include in your résumé.

Quite often, there are business councils or associations that relate to a specific ethnic group or region. You can search groups such as the Southeast Asia Canada Business Council and the Canada Caribbean Business Council on the Internet. They provide support services for small businesses, as well as business listings and information on importing and exporting, events to attend online or in person, and much more. You can also network with other successful business owners from your ethnic community and get information on starting a business in Canada. You may even get business leads from other members in the group.

The federal and provincial governments have many services, programs, and on-line resources available to help you start your business – from evaluating your idea to implementing it. Websites worth researching are www.canadabusiness.ca and the Ontario Government's Business link on the website **www.ontario.ca**.

One service to research is the Self-Employment Benefits Program funded by the Government of Canada. While a number of non-profit agencies administer the program, each has its own criteria. What they do, however, is to "help you take that seed of an idea and make it grow", and provide workshops and coaching services to help you succeed.

Other excellent government-funded resources are the Small Business Enterprise Centres that are available in various communities. They offer free workshops, computer and Internet access, consultations with qualified business consultants, business plan review, resource information, and they have an extensive reference library with business and association directories to help with your business and even job search.

Self-employment is a growing trend. It's both challenging and rewarding, but it takes hard work, self-motivation and discipline. If you would like to discover if you have what it takes to be self-employed, there's a great website, **www.mazemaster.on.ca/selfemployment/employment.htm**, which covers eight basic areas to consider when starting a business This site also has an on-line assessment tool to help you discover if you are capable of being your own boss, as well as other assessment tools related to your skills, interests and values. This can be accessed by the self-assessment link at the top of the home page.

A final tip to share, which can assist you in finding potential clients and even employers, is to network, and attend meetings and events that your prospective clients attend, especially if your target market is "business to business" (B2B).

Become a Consultant

Although some consultants are employed by consulting firms, many are self-employed and work from home. If you are considering self-employment, and you are an expert on a specific topic or process, and have a high level of specialized knowledge or skills, then offering your services as a consultant may help you earn the hourly rate that you are targeting. Keep in mind, though, that many consultants don't fill their weeks with billable work – you may earn more per hour as a consultant, but get paid for fewer hours per week - earning less overall than if you were an employee on salary.

Consulting, like other forms of self-employment, also gives you some flexibility in setting your schedule. This could be important if you have other responsibilities or need to combine work with school as you upgrade your education or work towards Canadian certification in your field. Consider combining part-time consulting in your field of expertise with part- or full-time employment in a "survival job" as you get established in the Canadian workplace.

Several researchers have identified factors that contribute to a consultant's success. Dr. Roberta Neault, president of Life Strategies Ltd. (a Canadian consulting firm), reviewed the research and identified specific personal characteristics, communication skills and business skills that are believed to be important for consultants. She gave permission to reproduce the "So You Want to be a Consultant?" checklist here for you:

So You Want to Be a Consultant?

Use this checklist to compare yourself with the Consulting Success Factors.

Step 1: Rate each factor according to the following scale

1 = Not at all like me   2 = A little like me   3 = Somewhat like me   4 = Quite like me   5 = Very much like me

Step 2: Identify, list and rank specific skills relevant to consulting expertise/niche

Step 3: Identify action steps to address/accommodate your lowest scores

Success Factor	Rating	Action Steps
Personal Characteristics		
Accountable		
Adaptable to any environment		
Analytical		
Comfortable without structure		
Commitment		
Continuously learning		
Credible		
Desire (to be a consultant)		
Energetic		
Entrepreneurial spirit		
Financial stability		
Flexible		
Focused on strengths		
Goal oriented		
Hard working		
Healthy		
Imaginative		
Independent spirit		
Life-long learner		
Making people feel at ease		
Marketable knowledge/expertise		
Multi-tasking		
Perceptive		
Persuasive		
Positive attitude		
Putting things in perspective		
Risk tolerant		
Self aware		
Self confident		
Self disciplined		
Self starter		
Strategic planner		
Supportive spouse		
Takes Initiative		
Tolerance for disappointment		
Tolerance for uncertainty		
Communication Skills		
Listening		
Questioning		
Speaking		
Writing		

Success Factor	Rating	Action Steps
Business Skills		
Attending professional meetings		
Attracting referrals		
Billing		
Computer		
Coordinating a board of advisors		
Identifying client needs		
Internet research		
Keeping records		
Maintaining extensive network		
Marketing		
Paying taxes		
Problem solving		
Time management		
Tracking expenses		
Writing reports		
Specific Expertise		
Other		

How to Interpret Your Results

If your total score is between 220 and 275, you likely have what it takes to be a successful consultant. Build on your strengths (your highest scores) and try to develop the characteristics that you scored lowest on. Consider partnering with others, hiring the skills you need and delegating specific tasks or only taking on the sections of consulting projects for which you are best suited.

If your score is between 165 and 219, you have some of the characteristics to be a successful consultant. However, you may find it helpful to work with someone else before taking on projects independently. Consider your lowest scores carefully and realistically assess whether these characteristics can be developed or if you should consider a different kind of work.

If your score is below 165, it means you haven't identified very many of the consulting success factors in your self-assessment. Consider asking a trusted friend or colleague to complete the checklist on your behalf, to see if he or she gets similar results. It's possible that you are not identifying strengths that others see in you. It's also possible that working as a consultant would not be a great fit; you may want to consider other options.

Explore Green Careers

This section is meant as an introduction to the emerging field of the "green economy" and "green careers", and not as an elaborate discussion of the topic.

As you contemplate your career options in Canada, and especially if you share a concern for environmental issues, you should look beyond traditional career paths and pay attention to the emerging "green' industry and the potential for green-collar jobs. Familiarize yourself with phrases like green economy, green jobs, green careers, solar power, clean energy, wind energy and renewable or sustainable energy. As a start, "green economy" refers to economic activity that improves the environment in some way and any position that ensures the well-being of the environment is a green job.

The green industry is one of the fastest growing segments of the job market, and continues to gain prominence as people become more concerned about protecting the environment, and as companies seek to be more socially responsible.

The transition to an environmentally-friendly green economy has the potential not only to replace lost jobs but also to limit the causes of environmental contamination and disasters. Finding a green job is no different from finding any other type of job. You will have to conduct research, assess your skills, and upgrade or learn skills that you lack.
Canada as a whole - and some of the provinces in particular - working on initiatives that will improve the environment and provide jobs in the sector. The Green Energy Act (of Ontario) received Royal Assent on May 14, 2009, with its major aims to:

- Spark growth in clean and renewable sources of energy such as wind, solar, hydro, biomass and biogas in Ontario.
- Create the potential for savings and better-managed household energy expenditures through a series of conservation measures.
- Create 50,000 jobs for Ontarians in its first three years.

Source: Ontario Ministry of the Environment:
http://www.mei.gov.on.ca/en/energy/gea/index.php

In addition, Seneca College in Toronto offers an 8-month bridging program called "Bridging to Green Careers". It is designed to help internationally trained immigrants succeed in Canada's environmental sector.

A sampling of green-career job resources and websites are:

- Canadian Wind Energy Association - **www.canwea.ca**
- Canadian Solar Industries Association - **www.cansia.ca**
- Environmental Careers Organization - **www.eco.ca**
- OYA Solar Inc. - **www.oyasolar.ca**
- People & Planet - **www.planetfriendly.net**
- The Green Pages - **www.thegreenpages.ca**
- Work Cabin - **www.workcabin.ca**
- Green Career Central - **www.Greencareercentral.com**
- Seneca College's Bridging to Green College - **http://www.senecac.on.ca/fulltime/BGC.html**
- International Environmental Job Listings - **www.environmentalcareer.info/index.asp**
- Environmental Jobs and Careers - **www.ecoemploy.com/**

As the concept of 'green' becomes more mainstream and as governments offer incentives to businesses to make them more competitive and environmentally friendly, there will be more opportunities for green-collar jobs. The following link will take you to a list of Canada's Greenest Employers: **http://www.canadastop100.com/environmental/**.

Experiment with Practice Firms
By Wayne Pagani

According to the Longitudinal Survey of Immigrants to Canada (LSIC), although 76 per cent of new immigrants have at least one type of international credential, 70 per cent experienced barriers in gaining access to the Canadian labour market at an appropriate level. **The biggest barrier to finding appropriate employment for immigrant professionals was the lack of Canadian work experience** (Source: *Statistics Canada, 2003b*).

Although the argument can certainly be made that Canada and Canadian employers have a long way to go in terms of seamless settlement and integration into the Canadian Labour Market, there are some resources and programs that can provide new immigrants with the opportunities to gain experience.

One such program is the Practice Firms (PF), which is a real office or workplace that simulates a business environment providing job seekers with an opportunity to gain real experience and develop their skills for specific occupations. It is estimated that there are currently over 5,000 practice firms worldwide. Many of these are associated with national or international networks of practice firms while others operate independently.

The Canadian Practice Firm Network (CPFN) explains that although practice firms are not yet very well known in Canada, they have had impressive results here since 1995. In Europe, practice firms originated over 50 years ago and are well known.

The first Canadian and North-American practice firm was opened in 1995 in Quebec City. The concept met with instant success, spreading throughout the Province of Quebec, and then throughout Canada. Today there are approximately 40 practice firms in Canada and their number is constantly on the rise, as new practice firms join the CPFN. For more information about the Canadian Practice Firm Network and a local practice firm in your area visit **www.rcee-cpfn.ca/** or call (418) 529-1384.

The practice firm within the CPFN develops and markets a variety of products or services, and then carries out transactions with thousands of its counterparts worldwide.

Publicity material, purchase orders, bills, and even cheques circulate throughout the international practice firm network. In a nutshell, everything conforms to reality except for the production and the delivery of goods, as well as the money used for the transactions.

Participants in a practice firm are unemployed persons or students. By carrying out their duties just as they would in a real firm, under the supervision of qualified staff members, they can acquire concrete professional experience in a real-office environment within an international trade context.

Furthermore, participants have the opportunity to develop their technical know-how, since part of their time is devoted to learning the most recent software programs and a second language. Finally, around 25 per cent of the practice firm's program involves job search activities, as the participants' ultimate goal is to get back into the job market as soon as possible.

Examples of independently-operated practice firms include Experica and Canadart.ca in Ottawa, Ontario. While both operate in bilingual settings, Experica is predominantly an English-speaking work environment while Canadart.ca is primarily French-speaking -. These two dynamic practice firms interact with each other in collaborating, conducting business, generating commercial activities and stimulating projects.

In this 12-week program, participants gain professional knowledge to develop their business skills and access employment opportunities while

"learning by doing". For more information, contact Experica at 613-688-3980 or **www.experica.ca**, and Canadart.ca at 613-744-1012 or **www.canadart.ca**

Typical positions available in practice firms include:

- Accounting
- Tech Support
- Applications Developer
- Administration
- Marketing
- Communication
- Purchasing
- Graphic Design
- Web Design
- Reception
- Human Resources
- Sales

The following are potential benefits of participating in a Practice Firm (for the job seeker):

- Gain Canadian experience in your field of expertise
- Become familiar with the nuances of Canadian business culture
- Participate in a business and team environment
- Improve skills by conducting meetings, leading projects, and fulfilling assigned job description
- Demonstrate competencies and ability to perform in the occupation being sought
- Learn the use of the latest in office software and technology
- Interact and share experiences with other job seekers in various fields (or departments)
- Earn a reference based on performance recognized by employers
- Engage in a structured return-to-work strategy with professional counselling and coaching
- Build confidence by improving your work habits and job search skills

Potential benefits of participating in a Practice Firm (for sponsors and companies in the Canadian Business Community):

- Get a well-trained workforce
- Lower recruitment costs
- Reduce the settling-in period
- Avoid errors when placing employees
- Effective system of assessment
- Provide good public relations opportunities

- Support the community in a practical way
- Free product/market research for products

In brief, a few weeks' stay in a practice firm is like taking part in an on-the-job training period with a firm, and receiving technical training while profiting from a program geared to help job seekers search for employment.

Practice Firm Success Stories

Louise Utamuriza
(Found employment with a local School Board)

"My time at Canadart was a great experience on both professional and personal levels. This allowed me to gain confidence in myself and assurance in my professional skills. I also took advantage of the job search tools offered to assist me in finding a job. I really appreciated the availability and the responsiveness of the coordinators. I recommend this program to anyone who might need it and I thank the team at Canadart for all they have done for me."

Marie Vonette Augustin
(Found employment as an HR Supervisor for a large multi-national chain store)

"I had just arrived in a country where I needed to learn and to discover almost everything on the cultural and professional levels. There was no question that I needed support and assistance to help me achieve my quest for success. Canadart, the Practice Firm, has been my springboard and taught me the necessary first steps towards success."

Safinaz El-halawani
(Found employment in various HR roles)

"I consider the Practice Firm experience to be extremely valuable to me because it provided practical experience in my profession. Experica gave me an opportunity to: refresh my current skills, learn about Canadian business practices, develop a career portfolio and gain a local work reference."

Olga Placinta
(Found employment as HR Administrator with Export Development Canada)

"I was very happy to have the opportunity to join Experica. Getting more hands on experience is one of the main goals but I would like to emphasize other benefits: Networking, exposure to different community events such as: career fairs, information interviews with real professionals within different fields; the professional expertise and advise from Employment Coordinators; amazing individuals are all part of [the] Experica experience. It is not a waste of time; it is a step closer to your personal and professional success. I am grateful for that experience and people that I met...they are my friends now."
I personally was able to land a job in my field through a career fair which I attended during my time at Experica."

CHAPTER 9

Navigating the Job Search Maze

Job Search Strategies for Success

These tips have already been covered in this book in various chapters, but they are so valuable and important for success that they are well worth repeating.

- **Know Yourself.** Make sure you have an idea of what your interests, values and skills are to enable you to begin a fruitful job search. Conduct an assessment to see what you enjoy doing and what workplace environment allows you to be more productive.

- **Evaluate Your "Soft Skills".** The majority of new employees fail in their jobs, not because of their technical abilities but because of poor interpersonal skills. You may know your job well, but that doesn't guarantee you success. Think about your soft skills – are you "coachable" and approachable? Can you accept and implement constructive feedback? How about your temper? Is your attitude friendly or miserable? Do you work well with others? Are you motivated to work at your full potential?

- **Be Diligent in Your Research.** Spend a great deal of your time conducting research on companies or industries that are of interest to you. Make sure you know what products or services each company provides and what position each company holds in the marketplace. In-depth research on a select group of companies is far better than randomly sending out hundreds of résumés and not getting any responses.

- **Create a Professional Profile.** This professional profile includes your résumé, which will most likely be your first point of contact with the employer. Make sure it showcases your accomplishments as they relate to the job for which you are applying, and that it focuses on the employer's needs and how you can fill those needs.

- **Be Honest.** As desperate as you may be to find a job, be truthful. Do not embellish your résumé with accomplishments that are not factual. Many people have been fired or have resigned in disgrace for such actions.

- **Ask for Help.** It is never a weakness to ask for support. Do you need assistance in getting an introduction to someone who could help you? Would you like to know how to arrange an informational interview to gain insights into certain companies or job functions? Do you need a job lead? Be courageous and ask for help. You may occasionally get a "No" answer but most people will be willing to lend a hand.

- **Give.** Do not hoard your knowledge, expertise, ideas or job leads. Be generous and share, because you will reap the rewards.

- **Network, Network, Network.** Begin to build your network of contacts by attending networking events that support your career goals, or join a professional association and become an active member. You must "work" the networking groups to which you belong as it's one of the most effective ways to find answers to your questions and find job opportunities.

- **Do Not Be Late.** Punctuality is highly valued in the workplace. Arrive 10-15 minutes before your scheduled meeting or interview. If possible, take a dry-run the day before your interview to give you an idea of how long it may take you to get there.

- **Mind Your Manners.** Be courteous to everyone you meet, whether in person or on the telephone. It is well known that some frontline staff wield a lot of influence and could stand in the way of your job search success. Remember common courtesies such as "please" and "thank you".

- **Maintain a Positive Attitude** even when things appear bleak. Tell yourself that the more "No's" you receive; the closer you are to "Yes," and remember that a quitter never wins.

- **Get Some Rest and Relaxation.** Job search is hard work, so take a break to avoid burn-out. Recharge your batteries. Get some exercise, do something with the family or just relax. You'll be surprised to see how rejuvenated you'll feel afterwards.

Seven Career SUCCESS Tips for Tough Times

"Create a vision and never let the environment, other people's beliefs, or the limits of what has been done in the past shape your decisions. Ignore conventional wisdom." - **Anthony Robbins, entrepreneur and author**

Right now, the world is experiencing an "economic tsunami", with job losses, bailouts, stimulus packages, oil spills...pretty despairing stuff. All this might have started in North America but the rippling effects are being felt around the world.

Perhaps you are one of those who have been laid off or you are feeling nervous because you don't know what's going to happen to your job. You may be getting ready to give up, but take a deep breath! Do not get too caught up into this *doom and gloom* frenzy. If you still have a job, find some creative ways to make yourself indispensable. If you have lost yours, then now is the time to think about other career possibilities. Read and apply any or all of these seven tips and you will be positioning yourself for **S.U.C.C.E.S.S.**:

Stop those ANTs in their tracks. Psychiatrist Daniel G. Amen refers to these ANTs as those **A**utomatic **N**egative **T**houghts that fill our heads most of the time - the Automatic Negative Thoughts that we engage in day-after-day with ourselves and with those around us. These are phrases like: "I can't find a job." "I am not good enough". "I am too old." "I don't have the experience." "Nobody ever gives me a break". "They won't hire me." "They already have someone hand-picked for the position." Do not feed into the negativities of the moment. Replace negative self-talk with positive and pragmatic conversation and, regardless of how things are going, try to maintain a state of positive expectation.

Understand that "this too shall pass". There's light at the end of this economic tunnel and you have the resilience to bounce back. It might be difficult at first as you may be overwhelmed and blinded by tears at times, but remember that depressions and recessions have come and gone and we have survived. Sometimes these upheavals happen to spark our creativity and get us out of places where we have become too comfortable. Now may be a good time to start that small business you have been thinking about, or go back to college to earn that degree or diploma you have been putting off. Look at these challenges as opportunities.

Communicate your value and your brand. Review your talents and preferences; determine what you are good at and what people say you do well. When it comes to your job search or your desire for a promotion, your résumé, education, and experience are not enough to influence the decision of a hiring manager. You need to communicate what you will bring to the table (your value) and how to package yourself in a way that will set you apart (your brand) from others vying for the same position. If you have a strong brand and you are able to articulate your value, you will attract employers, hiring managers and recruiters.

Commit to Change. It's often said that "change is the only constant" and, right now, we are witnessing lots of changes. Don't get stuck in the past and lament about what used to be, how things were done and what used to happen "back home". You have to be flexible, and learn to adapt and accommodate. One of the areas in which many people are resisting change is technology. If technology is a threat to your job or if your job was eliminated because of it, get up to speed and embrace this change because it's not going away. Take advantage of training programs sponsored by your company, look for opportunities to job-shadow a co-worker, or seek out opportunities to volunteer. Volunteering does not have to be only stuffing envelopes. There are many organizations looking for people with high-level skills to join committees or boards. Companies bent on showcasing themselves as good corporate citizens are giving their employees time during the workday to volunteer. Your next break could come via any of these routes.

Experience the Difference of having Experts on your Team. *"No man (or woman) is an island...no man (or woman) stands alone."* You cannot achieve your goals without the help of others, so develop your own *mastermind alliance* group that you can tap into for advice. These are experts whom you admire and who will hold you accountable to what you pledge to do. You should also develop, expand and leverage your support network as these individuals will be valuable to you when you are faced with a layoff or when changing careers. Seek them out wherever they are – in or outside your company – and start now! Don't wait until the layoff axe is hanging over your head. In leveraging your networks, remember that relationships take time to grow, so build and nurture them at every opportunity, not only in your time of greatest need.

Spotlight your Assets. You may be feeling so overwhelmed that asking you to spotlight your assets might be too much of a stretch right now, but this is a good place to begin. It takes your mind away from what you believe are your liabilities. So, first of all, learn to write things down. Keep a journal of your goals, special job achievements, awards and recognitions received, and positive comments made by your supervisor, coworkers or customers. These are your assets – documented evidence that validate your capabilities - and they will come in handy when you are ready to discuss a career path, or update or enhance your résumé.

Surround Yourself with Possibility Thinkers. Surround yourself with positive, uplifting, people – "possibility thinkers" who believe in themselves and in you. Possibility thinkers encourage, inspire and motivate you to move forward and go after what it is you want. This is where the seemingly impossible becomes possible! This is when you must move away from the naysayers and energy drainers, and advance towards those who constantly remind you that "Yes, you can!"

These tips will help you find some degree of **SUCCESS** as you move forward.

Real-Life Examples of Job Search Mistakes

How many times have you heard that "first impressions count?" Many job seekers believe that a professional résumé package is all that's required for a successful job search. They don't realize that an email address, the message on an answering machine or the inappropriate use of cell phones could give a hiring manager a negative impression.

The seven mistakes below are real situations taken from unsolicited emails actually received. The individuals are not clients so the element of confidentiality does not apply; however, their real identities are not used. Bloopers like these can severely derail a job search.

1. **Email Address**. Cute email addresses should be used only with your family and friends. They will not be considered *cute* by potential employers. All correspondence that pertains to your job search should have your real name or something that demonstrates professionalism. Consider the young woman who requested a critique of her résumé because she was not getting interviews. Her email address was **lazygirl@xxxxx.com**. This young lady was looking for a job in a restaurant. Why would an employer hire someone who is announcing that she is a "lazy girl"?

2. **Voicemail**. Your voicemail should convey your professionalism. In your absence, it becomes another tool to market yourself. Give yourself a call and listen to your message. Is it short, clear and businesslike? Don't be like this other young woman who wanted to know what she was doing wrong and why she couldn't find a job. Callers to her home heard a voicemail message that said "If you got this message, you may be someone I don't want to talk to, and if you are someone I don't want to talk to, you know what to do." Why would any hiring manager give her a second call after such a message?

3. **Résumé**. Don't be a part of the "cheating culture" by submitting someone else's résumé as if it's your own. That is never acceptable. In one particularly offensive situation, a man sent me an email asking to be hired. The name on his email address was different from the one he had as his signature, and the name on the résumé was also different. Three aliases! When the recipient contacted him, suggesting that he decides who he really is, his reply was "*u think i am dumb?*"

4. **Cover Letter**. Take the time to write a proper, professional cover letter to accompany your résumé whether you are applying by email or sending it by snail mail (regular postal service). Your cover letter is another opportunity to market yourself to the employer; a chance to draw attention to your special skills or to something that was not covered in your résumé. The majority of hiring managers still want to see a cover letter whether or not the job posting asks for only a résumé.

5. **Interview**. Your résumé and cover letter brought you to this important stage. It is now time for you to shine; to tell the interviewer why you are the best candidate for the job. It's inevitable that you are going to hear the question "Do you have questions?" You should be prepared with a few good ones. One young man answered, "No", then went home and sent an email with a long list of questions to the interviewer.

6. **Job Offer**. If you have reached the stage where you have been offered the job, it means the company really wants you. While it is normal, and sometimes expected, that a certain amount of negotiation will take place, don't blow your chances by asking for the impossible. One young man, fresh out of graduate school, thought he should push the envelope by informing the interviewer that the other company was offering him much more money. He lost on both fronts as this company could not match the offer and he did not have an offer from the other company.

7. **Cell Phone**. Watch your cell phone manners. One of the last things you do before going into an interview is to turn off your cell phone. Do not put it on vibrate, but turn it off. Not only will it be embarrassing to you if it rings during the interview, but it could spell disaster to your job search. An HR manager told the story of a salesman who, wanting to impress his potential employer, took a call from his manager during the interview and calmly told him he was meeting with a client.

Your job search is much more than a résumé and cover letter. It's a package of professionalism starting with your first contact with the company. Overlooking proper job search etiquette could be detrimental to your career success.

The Role of Employment Agencies and Recruiters

In your job search, employment (or staffing) agencies are your allies. They provide a gateway to a company as well as provide you with an opportunity to test the waters and determine whether or not you would want to work at specific companies. Of course, working with an agency provides an opportunity to begin your "Canadian experience". When you work through an employment agency, you are paid by the agency, not the company where you work. You are not required to pay any fees to the agency as they are paid by the company.

Recruiters or *headhunters* are other sources to contact for assistance with your job search. These individuals work with companies to find qualified candidates and are paid by the companies. They do not work for the candidate. However, if a recruiter finds a candidate that would be a good fit for the company, he or she will do everything to market that candidate to the company. Because recruiters know the key decision-makers in certain companies, it is a good idea to meet these individuals and develop a strong relationship with them. This does not mean you should be calling them every day as they will see you as a nuisance and will not want to help you.

The Hiring Manager's Perspective
By Tanya Sinclair

What do employers and recruiters pay attention to when looking at résumés? When initially screening résumés, employers and recruiters look for those that match the job they are seeking to fill. They also look for any "red flags" or questions that are left unanswered after reviewing the entire résumé. Some things to consider:

1. Is the résumé easy to read, neat and professional?
2. Are there spelling or grammatical errors?
3. What education and experience does the applicant list that would suggest they have the knowledge, skills and abilities required to perform the job?
4. Did the applicant take time to customize the résumé to target this particular job or industry?
5. Are there any gaps in employment history from one job to the next?
6. Has the applicant changed jobs frequently? After short periods of time?
7. Does the applicant show signs of career progression or simply shifting to lateral or lower-level positions?

Additional information on what recruiters and hiring managers look for in a résumé can be found in **Appendix II & III** gathered from the 2010: Canadian Résumé and Interview Trends survey conducted by The Wright Career Solution.

Employee Referral Programs: Many companies are using employee referral programs to increase the number of qualified candidates. Employees are often willing to refer people they know, especially if there is a reward attached. Ask people you know if they have this type of program at their workplace. Pass along your résumé and ask them to refer you for jobs in their company.

Applicant Tracking Systems (keywords): Several organizations receive such a high volume of applicants that they use résumé database programs to find résumés with keywords that match skills, credentials and experience they need for each role. When uploading your résumé to apply online, be sure to include the keywords from the job posting in your résumé.

Never Embellish Your Résumé

There is one particular website that promotes lying about the places you have worked, degrees that you have attained, and provides references that you don't know. While many people lie about their skills, education and job experiences on their résumés, you don't want to do it. It's easy for employers to find out the truth about you, and you don't want to start out on the wrong path.

Résumé frauds range from exaggerated skills or duties at a previous job, a concealed termination or inflated education qualification. Below are some examples of people who inflated their qualifications in order to get jobs or secure positions.

- **"Official Résumé Wrong"** was the headline in the sports section of a popular newspaper a few years ago, when it was discovered that the then manager of a certain major league baseball team had inaccuracies in his bio. Although he played with a professional baseball team he was not an "All-American basketball player" neither did he play basketball for one of the leading US universities, as he said. When asked by a sportswriter, the manager admitted the statements were incorrect and said he should be judged by what he does on the field, not by what's written about him.

- Some time ago, it was reported in newspapers and on the Internet that an individual who was planning to purchase a football team had to revise his Fact Sheet because it contained numerous errors. He did not play in the National Football League nor the Canadian Football League, neither did he play in the Little League World Series when he was 11 years old. He has a degree in social work, not "a degree in Business Administration with an emphasis on Finance" as his original bio claimed.

Do these incidents only happen in sports? No! There have been occasions where individuals have been caught misrepresenting themselves as doctors, lawyers or professors. One man practiced medicine in the US and Canada for 10 years before it was found out he never had a medical degree. A federal politician had to resign when it was revealed he never attended law school as he claimed on his résumé.

The offenders are not always men, if you are beginning to wonder. A former politician in Canada resigned from her position because she inflated her academic and professional credentials when she claimed to have been "working as a visiting professor at Princeton".

Studies carried out by a reference-checking firm in Toronto some years ago found that 27 per cent of applicants embellished their educational backgrounds; 25 per cent lacked job knowledge, and 19 per cent were dismissed or not eligible for rehire. The company randomly selected 1,000 job applicants, ranging from general office workers to senior executives, on whom they had conducted reference checks and education verifications. They found that 35 per cent of these candidates presented "red flags".

We live in a very competitive marketplace – too few jobs for too many employees. As such, it is tempting to twist facts, but before you decide to exaggerate your skills, education and experience, think of the consequences when the truth is known.

If you were fired from your previous job, it is best to be honest about it. If you worked on a project as part of a team, don't give the employer the impression you did it alone. If you are enrolled in a program, don't say you already earned the degree or diploma. Employers want to know who you are and what you have done with your talents, but do not exaggerate the facts to gain an edge over other candidates.

Learn to Listen!

> *"Knowledge speaks, but wisdom listens."* – **Jimi Hendrix, well-known musician**

Learning to listen while going about your job search is very important. Sometimes we are so focused on what we want to say that we take over the conversation and leave little or no time for the other people to say anything. That urge to talk rather than listen can cause us to miss some valuable opportunities.

Effective listening is a skill that requires practice, much like playing tennis. One person serves while the other prepares to receive. One person speaks; the other listens. Unfortunately when we fail to listen, it can alter the person's message and we end up missing the point. The following tips will assist you in improving your listening skills:

- **Create Rapport.** Begin to build a relationship of trust as people are drawn to people that they like and trust. Look directly at the person. Smile and nod to show that you are genuinely interested in what's being said.

- **Screen out all Distractions.** Give the person your undivided attention. Make sure you have turned off your cell phone, for example. This is the time to focus entirely on the person speaking. This tells them that you respect and value their opinion.

- **Be Prepared.** Keep a pad and pencil close at hand to jot down notes. This shows that you are engaged and business-like, and gives you a chance to review the notes and ask for clarification.

- **Do not Interrupt.** Sometimes you may be tempted to throw in your own thoughts or finish the sentence, probably because it's a subject matter that you know a whole lot about or you have heard the story before. Instead of interrupting, listen attentively and act as if you are hearing it for the first time.

- **Rephrase and Clarify**. Rephrase what the person has said to show that you are paying attention. "So, are you saying that the only downside to this job is the amount of traveling that's involved?" If you are able to recap or rephrase the person's words, it gives them an opportunity to clarify and say exactly what they mean. As well, they will feel flattered that you took the time to listen and you will have had another opportunity to hear exactly what was said.

Telephone Etiquette

The telephone plays a very important part in your job search. After you have sent your résumé, the telephone will most likely be your next point of contact. You will need to make sure that everyone in your household knows that you are actively looking for work and that anyone could be calling to arrange an interview. Make sure everyone answers the telephone in a professional manner.

As mentioned before, when you are job searching, it's not the time to be cute with your voicemail. Messages that are weird or funny will not impress a potential employer when she calls. If you have voicemail or an answering machine, ensure that your message is clear, short and polite. Instead of using the automated messaging system that comes with your telephone service, record a personal message such as:

You have reached the voicemail of Harry Evans. I am not available to speak with you at this time. Please leave me a short message with your name and telephone number and I will return your call shortly.

When you are recording the message, make sure you are standing as it allows for clarity and a better tone. After you have recorded the message, use the replay feature to listen. Is your message clear? Does it give the impression that you're smiling? Are there any background noises?

If you receive someone's voicemail when you call, leave a message that is clear and short. Include your name, your telephone number, and the reason for your call. Here is a sample message:

Hello Betty, I am Jose Vargas. I understand from Stan Holmes that you are looking for a translator who is able to communicate in Spanish, English and French. I am fluent in all three languages and currently work as a translator for a community organization in Toronto. I would appreciate if you could return my call at (905) 555-0012 to discuss how I might be able to assist you. Again, my name is Jose Vargas and I can be reached at (905) 555-0012.

Note the repetition of the person's name and phone number at the end of the message. This allows the listener another opportunity to get the name and number without having to replay the message.

Be Prepared for Job Layoffs

"One of the secrets of life is to make stepping stones out of stumbling blocks."
– **Jack Penn, American author**

Depending on your country of origin, you may be accustomed to situations where a person joins a company and remains there until retirement. Layoffs, downsizing or rightsizing are quite common in the Canadian workplace, and it should not be a surprise if you obtain a job with a company and find yourself laid off within a year.

One recent example saw a number of prominent Canadian companies laying off thousands of employees for a variety of reasons ranging from "maintaining a tighter rein on costs" to creating "a simpler, nimbler organization." Although the news is usually shocking, layoffs don't just happen suddenly. There are usually subtle signs that changes are coming. While you should not become paranoid with the thought, you should keep an eye out for tell-tale signs, and be prepared to handle such eventualities. Here are some tips to help with your preparation:

- **Keep an eye out for any news about the company.** Was there a sudden departure of its senior management ranks? Are there dramatic fluctuations of its share price? Is there an exodus of many of its core employees? The answers to these questions will be a good indicator of where your company is heading.

- **Take advantage of learning opportunities offered by the company.** These may be formal training where you attend classes outside of work or free in-house courses offered such as lunch-and-learn programs. Don't forget the Internet, which provides a variety of learning opportunities. Although your job may appear safe at the moment, you shouldn't stop learning.

- **Be on the lookout for internal vacancies and assess yourself to see if your skills match the requirements.** Speak with someone within the department where there is a vacancy to gather additional information about the position and then submit your application.

- **Find out if there are opportunities to job-shadow another employee or be cross-trained on a system**. Such initiatives will help to prepare you for your next career move, whether within or outside the company.

- **Make yourself indispensable** (at least give it a try) by keeping abreast of industry developments. Arrange informational interviews to learn more about a field you are interested in or to keep current with trends in your industry. Watch, listen to and read the news, and see if you can use any of the knowledge gained to enhance your current position.

- **Start a journal of your special achievements, comments made by your supervisor or co-workers, and awards and recognitions received.** Review your performance appraisals. What did your supervisor say about you? Did you work on a special project? Were you a member of a team that developed a system which added to the company's profitability? These notes will come in handy when you are ready to update your résumé.

- **Develop and nurture a network of contacts, even if you're not looking for a job.** Many people have the misconception that networking is done only when one is job hunting. It is an ongoing process; it takes time to grow, but will be valuable when faced with a layoff or when changing careers.

- **Join a professional association and contribute.** You'll learn new skills, meet new people and build credibility among your peers. Many organizations send their job postings to some of these associations before they reach the newspapers. Saying that you are a member of a professional association will add to your credibility.

- **There might be someone whom you admire in or outside your company.** Ask if you could discuss your uncertainties or your career plans with them. It's not a weakness to ask for help.

After being in one job for a while, a layoff, though uninvited, may just be what you need to propel you to action; to change careers; to do something different. Redirect your energy into something productive and don't feel sorry for yourself.

CHAPTER 10

Stories That Inspire

"Embrace the culture of the country where you live. Sports is a great way to do it without giving up your identity." – **Rajesh Subrananiam, Executive at FedEx Canada**

The quote above embodies the essence of becoming fully involved in your adopted home and ties in with the short stories introduced in this section. Some people have succeeded against all odds; others have returned to - or are contemplating returning to - their home countries; others are still trying to find their way through the transition maze.

The following stories are provided here to give you a glimpse of what others who have come before you have experienced and what they have done to circumvent the obstacles in their paths. Some of the names have been changed or withheld by request but the stories are real.

My Story...

"... Are you close to quitting? Please don't do it. Are you discouraged? Hang in there. Are you pessimistic about your job? Roll up your sleeves and go at it again". - **Max Lucado, Minister of Religion**

My story is not so much about me as it is about giving you hope; about another immigrant just like you, faced with uncertainties just like you: someone who wasn't about to give up at the first sign of negativity in the workplace but, more importantly, someone who believes in persevering and going after her dreams.

It's a story to tell you that "you can do it"; to encourage you to see obstacles as opportunities...every time! These experiences have strengthened me. Without them, I would've become complacent. I would've sat in the same job year after year, being sorry for myself. Without them, I wouldn't be driven to write this book. I also recognise that, through it all, I have met, worked with, and worked for some wonderful people who clearly saw what I brought to the table.

When I returned to Canada in 1989 (having landed in 1988), and started my job search, I did not hear "No Canadian Experience" but at the time I attributed it to the fact I had had "American Experience," having secured a job with the United Nations in New York while en route to Canada from Jamaica.

My first Canadian experience started with an employment agency through which I did temporary assignments. Some assignments lasted one week, others two or three days, but my first permanent job came a month after I began my search and it was through networking. My friend's husband knew someone at a company who was looking for administrative help. I stayed there all of three weeks as the repetitive task of typing purchase orders became too much of a no-brainer.

"Being defeated is often a temporary condition. Giving up is what makes it permanent". – **Marlene vos Savant, inspirational author**

My next permanent job was with one of the "Big Six Banks" and that opportunity came five months after I had arrived in Canada. While there, I enrolled in the Public Administration degree program at Ryerson on a part-time basis. After five years at the bank, it had become evident that I had reached the proverbial glass ceiling. My performance appraisals were stellar, yet I felt stuck, stifled and fed up. It was obvious I was being passed over for promotions, and when I asked for feedback I heard I was "a close second". Never one to be defeated, I started looking for opportunities outside the bank.

The idea to start a part-time business offering résumé writing and business services came to mind. At the same time, I sent my résumé to the colleges in the Greater Toronto Area, to explore any teaching opportunities, as I had had some teaching experience. I received a call from Sheridan College almost immediately to say they didn't have any vacancies at the time, but would keep my résumé on file. I could easily have given up, but six months later I followed up with a telephone call and was invited for an interview.

Two weeks after the interview, I became a part-time professor in the Faculty of Business teaching in the Executive Administration Program. This new career direction entailed negotiating with the bank to change my employment status from full-time to part-time, an arrangement that lasted for six months. I decided to concentrate on my part-time business and teaching.

Eighteen months later, downsizing hit the college and part-time teachers were the first targets. I decided to return to the corporate world, but did temporary work to give me the flexibility to continue with my part-time business. One company hired me on contract for a maternity leave replacement of eight months and, when the incumbent opted not to return, I was offered the job. I negotiated with the employer to work three days a week because I was intent on operating my part-time business.

It became apparent after a while that senior management wanted a full-time person in the position, so I trained my successor and left - not knowing what I was going to do, other than continue with the part-time business. One month after I left, I was networking at a meeting of a professional organization and learned of a position at another company. I applied for the position and was hired.

I will be forever indebted to some of the people I worked with at these companies. They recognized the value I brought to the organizations, supported my continuing education and career goals, and gave me the flexibility to do my job.

I will fast forward to my current status as a self-employed career development practitioner. I believe wholeheartedly in self-development and, for me, it meant attending school. After completing the Public Administration degree, I contemplated pursuing an MBA program but switched gears as I believed my time and effort would be better spent helping others with their careers. After all, I had changed careers a number of times and people were coming to me for advice on how they could change theirs if they got stuck. I enrolled in the post-graduate Career Development program at Conestoga College.

This is my calling, this is my mission. Has it been easy? No! Is it achievable? Yes!

It would be remiss of me not to pay tribute to the two countries that have made all this possible.

To Jamaica, the land of my birth, where it was ingrained in me from an early age that obstacles are opportunities waiting to be explored.

To Canada, O Canada, which has given me the opportunity to explore. If I had to do it all over again, I would still make the same decision, but with a clearer understanding of what lies ahead.

I hope my story, along with those of the other contributors, will remind you that your present circumstance is just for a short time. It will get better if you continue to persevere.

The late US President Lyndon B. Johnson said during the civil rights era of the 60s that *"We must not only open the doors of opportunity, but we must also equip our people to walk through those doors."* I am turning around that quote to say to employers: *"The new immigrant is already equipped. Open the doors and give him or her an opportunity."*

Their Stories...

Keith Forde, Retired Deputy Chief of Police, Toronto Police Service

"Perseverance seldom fails." That's the philosophy of Retired Deputy Chief Keith Forde, who was destined to be a police officer from the age of eight in his native Barbados. He wanted to "serve without fear or favour" but did not get much encouragement from his parents.

Instead of joining the force in Barbados, he went to Montreal in 1969, where he enrolled at Sir George William Business School. He still dreamt of becoming a police officer and, although he didn't see any black officers in Montreal, he made enquiries about joining that force. He was told he had to be bilingual and his hopes were dashed.

However, while attending a friend's wedding in Toronto, he saw a couple of black officers and decided to apply to the Toronto Police Force in 1972, and he was accepted. Today, he is the force's first Black to hold the position Deputy Chief, and head of Human Resources. In this role, one of his mandates was to make sure that the Toronto Police Service reflected the demographics of the public it serves – a challenging task, but one that he was more than equipped to handle.

Deputy Chief Forde, like many new immigrants, had his share of obstacles along the way, but he persevered. He kept focussed on his goals – where he wanted to go. *"Those obstacles strengthened my resolve,"* he said. He believes that although there are lots of challenges, opportunities abound in this country. But for new immigrants to function effectively, they need to know how the society functions and how to access services.

He advises new immigrants not to wait for things to happen but make them happen. In reference to Ontario as one of the main urban centres where new immigrants choose to settle, the Deputy Chief said: *"If you can't make it in Ontario, you can't make it anywhere else."*

Teresa Gonzales, translator from Cuba

Teresa is a former translator from Cuba. Although she spoke a bit of English, the fact that she could not understand most of what people were saying made it quite stressful to be in a group. She was directed to a non-profit organization where she participated in a one-week self-marketing program. The program introduced her to a structured approach to developing résumés and cover letters, and how to prepare for interviews.

It was a new experience as, in her country, there was no formal job search process. She enrolled in a computer training program and attended English as a Second Language classes. Six months after completing her classes she applied for the vacant position of administrative assistant with the same non-profit organization and was successful.

Her job entails answering the telephones and taking minutes at meetings. She was frightened, doubted herself sometimes, but vowed to do all it took to succeed at the job. She visited the public library, borrowed tapes, learned phrases, and watched English programs on television. She also received a lot of support from her co-workers. Initially, it was easy for her to meet with other Spanish-speaking coworkers but found that her English skills were not being developed quickly, so she forced herself to integrate with English-speaking co-workers as often as she could. This helped to improve her English language skills.

Teresa's advice to other newcomers to Canada is to learn English, and French, if possible. She also advises them to be prepared to adjust. Have a goal and create steps that lead to the goal. She was fortunate to land a job within six months of arriving in Canada, but it does not happen often, and newcomers should be prepared to start at an entry-level position, if that's the first opportunity to come their way.

Mr. Marsh, energy savings consultant

While in my lawyer's office in New York in 1998 contemplating registering a business in the US, the lawyer asked me if I knew that Canada had a program for internationally-trained engineers. I didn't know, but it sounded interesting and I knew I would qualify because I have a Masters in Electro-Mechanical Engineering obtained at the St. Petersburg Polytechnic University in Russia. On hearing such good news, I changed my plans and, months later, my family and I were on our way to Canada, to get one of those engineering jobs.

Our home, for the first four nights, was a hotel because we didn't have anyone to stay with. We immediately started looking for a place to live, school for our children, and a place of worship. I also needed to open a bank account and, since I had already established an account with a subsidiary of one of Canada's major banks, I walked into one of its branches. However, I was told I needed to open an account and wait three weeks to access the funds.

Fortunately. I met someone who introduced me to the superintendent at the apartment complex where I was going to live. My knowledge of Russian came in handy as I had to explain to this individual that I wanted to open a bank account. He referred me to the Ukrainian Credit Union and, in minutes, I had established an account and walked out with cash in hand.

As for the job scene, I soon realized that it was not going to be easy for me to get a job as an engineer. Within six months, we had used up all the money we had taken and, while I continued with my job search, my wife found one in a call centre paying $10 per hour. Months later, I resigned myself to taking a job in a factory, driving pallet trucks and packing skids at $10 per hour as well. I knew this was not where I belonged, so I decided to explore new avenues.

I heard about the federally-funded Experienced Worker Program that could assist me in starting a business, but, once I did the research, I found out it was not that easy. However, I was led to the OPTIONS program which was a partnership between OACETT (Ontario Association of Certified Engineering Technicians & Technologists) and a non-profit agency. I went through the program and was hired by a company to provide energy consultancy services. I worked with them until the government discontinued the program. I am now in the midst of starting my own energy-savings business."

Mr. Marsh's Advice

If you are over 40, have the experience and qualifications, and you would like to remain in your field, my advice is to stick with your core skills. Look for short-term practical courses and seminars that will enhance your qualifications and offer you a Canadian certificate. Then continue to search for opportunities in your field. In order to put food on the table and pay the bills, you may have to take a survival job, but it doesn't mean it is the end of your career. Keep going and never deviate from your goal.

If you are under 40 and qualified and you are running into obstacles, I would suggest that you return to school. You have enough time to get into the system and learn as much as you can. Becoming an apprentice in the skilled trades could be a very good alternative because of the shortage of skilled labour in the Canadian job market and the potential to earn a reasonably high income.

Estela Alvarez, former advertising professional from Colombia

Estela and her husband both worked in advertising in Colombia. Her first Canadian job was as a volunteer in a call centre, but it was extremely difficult as her English skills were not great. She went through a self-marketing program, and found it very useful. She heard of a vacancy at a non-profit organization for a program assistant and sent out her first and only résumé. She was selected from a total of 234 applicants and refers to the experience as "a miracle." Estela believes she was successful because of the confidence she has in herself.

Estela says that "sometimes we create our own barriers". She encourages people to believe in themselves, approach every situation with an open mind and take advantage of every opportunity that's available for new immigrants.

Elizabeth, communication/PR specialist: Beating the odds in the Canadian job search

I arrived here from the Caribbean several years ago, after what I thought was a well-planned transition to settle in a land of promise. Not so much for me, but for my then six-year-old son.

Soon after I arrived in Canada I began to look for a job – anything – which could utilize the skills I had acquired as a communications professional over the 16+ years of my career, and use that job as a launching pad for a number of ambitious things.

Although I had passed the 40-year threshold, I thought these plans were entirely possible. I was able-bodied, had a reasonably good education up to university level, I spoke excellent English, had been fully Westernized and accustomed to the North American way of life; I could use a computer and I had a heck of a lot of career experience under my belt.

By my estimation, without the much vaunted "Canadian experience" and in full knowledge of the fact that I was competing in a marketplace chock full of other immigrants, I gave myself six months to find some kind of employment in Canada. I was fully resigned to the fact that I would probably not gain employment commensurate to the level I had attained back home.

I began my job search in earnest. My friend, who is a reputable career coach, ensured that my résumé was saying the right things, and I began to network as a means of getting job leads. I also registered with a few employment agencies.

Two months into my job search, I accepted a one-day assignment as a receptionist at a small engineering company. I had earned a full seven hours of "Canadian experience!"

I began to seek volunteer opportunities, which I was told was one way to earn 'Canadian experience,' so, in my fourth month of job search, I found a volunteer opportunity with a humanitarian aid agency. The work was basic but I was using the computer, honing my skills on some frequently used software programs and, of course, racking up my Canadian experience portfolio. I saw a posting for a permanent position (intermediate) within that same organization and gleefully applied for it. I applied through the normal channel and got in for an interview...well prepared. Oops, midway through interview, I was diplomatically told that perhaps I was "overqualified' for the position. The end result was that I was not successful as they were looking for "the right fit".

Not only did I now have to deal with having "no Canadian experience" but I was also now "overqualified" for jobs. Four or five interviews later, I still heard the same refrain. I began to see this process as a challenge and, in fact, as a battle of the wits because there always seems to be a way to stack the odds against persons who are new to the Canadian marketplace, even if they speak impeccable English and are fully acculturated.

I stepped up my job search operations by scheduling some informational interviews as a means of not only getting leads but also understanding what makes up the Canadian workplace. So, while frustration and the temptation to go back home seemed an attractive alternative, I continue to knock on doors, hoping to "get my foot in the proverbial door".

While I await an encounter with some enlightened person who is attuned to the reality that technology has opened up the world in such a way that different cultures and norms are no longer strangers with each other, I will use the time to gain even more skills and knowledge, and ultimately more confidence. Then clichés like "no Canadian experience" and "overqualified" will become so passé that people will begin to see them for what they really are – lame excuses for refusing great talents.

Carlos, medical doctor from Cuba

"Canadian experience? It makes me laugh, because every time I hear that I think of a friend of mine when he went to apply for a job. This guy has a deep knowledge of the most common programs created by Microsoft and the post he was applying for required that. The first thing he was asked was if he had any Canadian experience, to which he replied, *"Do you know that Microsoft is an American company?"*

After some time thinking about the real meaning of that question, I have realized that what the employer really wants to know is if the prospective employee has been domesticated, in the same sense that someone domesticates a wild animal, to obey every single command given, and not be rebellious.

My profession is in the "health industry", a category denomination that sounds highly commercial; two words that don't really match each other. I am not able to practice in Canada due to regulations in this field, but neither in almost any other because as soon as someone is aware of your qualifications they give you the "overqualified speech" and then you know that this is the end of the interview.

Everybody présumés that "if you haven't done it in Canada you don't know how to do it". There are really things that are done differently here, but this is not a whole different world.

What is left to do probably is to downgrade your qualification and experience in the next interview for a job that really doesn't have anything to do with your body of knowledge and skills. In this way you find a lot of highly qualified individuals doing jobs for which almost no qualification is needed. I understand now why there is so much resentment amongst some of the people I have met since I came to Canada. It has started to affect me now.

Edward Ndububa from Nigeria

I arrived in Canada in 1979 from Nigeria on a scholarship to George Brown College just after graduating from high school. I was to pursue a program in Electronics Engineering Technology and return to Nigeria. Instead, the government extended the scholarship, and I moved to New Brunswick where I graduated with a degree in Education and one in Electrical Engineering.

I then did a Masters in Electronics and Robotics at Indiana State University and returned to Canada in September 1988. Although I had done post-secondary studies here in Canada, I was still unable to find a job in my field, so I took a job sorting flowers and was paid CDN$7.50 per hour. After one month, I began driving the delivery truck taking flower sellers to street corners and picking them up in the evenings. I did that for three months.

My next venture was to sell encyclopaedias as I had heard "there was money to be made" in such a business. I was not making any money, but each place I visited I would continue to drop off my résumé. On one of my "encyclopaedia" trips, the owner of an electronics company saw my résumé and asked if I "was really that qualified." He offered me a job paying $8.50 per hour. I didn't have anything to lose as I had not made any money selling these books.

My job was to fix remote controls. I continued to search for jobs in my field, and after four months, I received three job offers with Nortel, Hewlett Packard and a contractor with the Department of Defence. I chose Nortel and began working with them in March 1989.

I moved around, and was promoted through different departments at Nortel, and after more than 10 years, one of my colleagues invited me to join her and another fellow to start a company, named SS8 Networks Inc. It grew beyond our ability to effectively handle it and we were out-manoeuvred by one of California-based venture capital companies.

In 2002 I started SGNT Technologies, a company that specializes in providing outsourcing services in hardware and software development as well as delivering a rich portfolio of information technology (IT) products and services from brand-name manufacturers and partners.

My advice to any new Canadian is, *"never give up even though the situation looks bleak. Keep focused on your goal. Eventually that door of opportunity is going to swing open. Be persistent!"*

Shifali Jain, human resources professional

My young daughter and I arrived in Canada from India in 2004 to reunite with my husband. It was very difficult for me as I had a Master's degree in Human Resources and was well established in my career. But because family came first, I decided to give up what I had and come to Canada.

I was unable to find work in my field as there were quite a few barriers and I was initially depressed. I then found out about ACCES Employment Services, a 20-year community-based employment organization that offers employment counselling to new Canadians over the age of 25.

Through this organization I learned of The Mentoring Partnership and was paired with an experienced mentor at CIBC bank who helped me to establish contacts and learn about the Canadian workplace. That relationship made all the difference. Early in 2006, two years after I arrived in Canada, I was employed as a human resources professional with CIBC.

ACCES paved the way for me to broaden my horizons, and I thank them for their program.

My advice to any new immigrant in a similar situation as I was:

> *"Reach out and tell people you need help; understand the society and the work culture; remain focused; it's never too late to learn or to start over. Your goal is attainable...just hang in there."*

Helen: My experiences and recommendations

I was an associate professor in Economics at one of the Ukrainian universities. I was in the USA affiliated with the University of Kansas for one year, where I taught a course and had an internship at one of the state departments.

Upon my return to the Ukraine I got five years experience as a project manager working on projects with international organizations such as KPMG, Ericsson, the USAID and UNDP.

When I came to Canada, upon consultations with my friends who arrived earlier, I decided that I had to upgrade my skills and get a better understanding of the Canadian market through post-graduate studies at a college.

I conducted labour market research so I could compare different opportunities in terms of career perspectives and comparative advantages of different programs. My choice was marketing management. I entered George Brown College to pursue a one-year postgraduate program with a co-op component.

It was difficult to get the right co-op, but I managed to find one myself due to initiative, sharing experiences with my classmates and taking their advice. I got a job while I was still at the college, but it did not last long partly due to the cultural differences between the employer's expectations and mine. After a few months I was laid off.

I started looking for another position, but there were several factors preventing me from landing a position. On one hand, I was a mature person with good project management and analytical experience, but on the other, I did not have enough Canadian experience.

I heard about the Career Bridge program from one of my friends, and I applied immediately. My diplomas were already evaluated and I registered with the program in the summer of 2005. I was fortunate to be selected for an internship within the Career Edge organization. After two months, I was offered a full-time contract position.

Some of my recommendations for foreign-trained professionals are:

- Do labour market research, and come up with a plan.
- Evaluate your hard and soft skills to see what's lacking, then search for opportunities to gain the necessary skills.
- Do not limit yourself by sending out lots of résumés and cover letters. This is the passive way and it is unlikely that it will bring you success. Instead, do cold calls and go out to meet people in your field, either through professional organizations, or by arranging informational interviews.
- Try to get in touch with people of your nationality who have their own businesses. Ask them to take a look at your résumé, and tell you where to go to get more information and meet other professionals in your field.
- Go to the church and community services centres where you can find printed materials. You may be lucky to meet the right person who can give you some good advice on your résumé, cover letter and job opportunities.
- Analyze the response rate you are getting on your résumé and cover letter, and improve it according to the job requirements. Try to understand exactly what the employer is looking for and address the requirements in your marketing documents.

- Improve your conversation skills by joining a community group and tell people that you are looking for a good conversation group.
- Be positive. Try to enjoy life in its small and big details. Looking for a job is hard and you need to have enjoyable moments in your life to lessen the pressure.
- Develop friendships with people who are willing to morally support you.
- Use Career Bridge or The Mentoring Partnership programs – two of the best programs designed to assist internationally-educated professionals.
- Be persistent and self-confident.

Experience of a teacher immigrating to Canada

I had a stable job as a teacher and a Master's degree in a developing Third World country, so when I made the decision to migrate to a First World country I thought I would've landed the ideal job on arrival. I was up for one of the biggest surprises of my professional career.

Based on the invitation that Canada extends to professionals, I never thought that the whole experience would be so frustrating and frightening. At the time I made the decision (2002), it was never mentioned that certification from the Ontario College of Teachers was a mandatory requirement to teach in the Ontario school system; neither was I told I would need to obtain a Canadian Criminal Record check. To make matters worse, I needed to be living in Canada for at least six months before I could apply for this record check. It therefore meant that, with bills to be paid and food to be eaten, I had to seek some means of employment. Having a young child to care for, too, I had no choice but to take on a survival job that just barely allowed ends to meet.

The other frustrating part of the experience was that every interview that I went for, clerical or otherwise, I was told that I needed Canadian experience. At this point, I started regretting my decision to leave my country, but something kept telling me to fight it out until I could get into my profession. With this new frame of mind, I decided to volunteer at a high school to obtain some added experience in the classroom as well as for the networking opportunities. I did this for five months while still working at the survival job.

With all these setbacks, walking the mall became a regular therapy to relieve some of my stress. One day, I came upon a community services exhibition, which addressed professional immigrants and there I was told about a mentoring program. After going to the meeting and being assigned a mentor, life for me became a bit more bearable as I was given lots of guidance and encouragement which I needed to keep me going.

I kept the faith, stuck with the trials – which were many – and went back to school for six months to get an extra credit for the teaching certification.

After two years of waiting, I finally got the provisional certification from the Ontario College of Teachers (OCT), which certified me to teach in Ontario schools. This was the ticket I needed to start applying for teaching jobs, but there were more obstacles.

I went for six interviews at six different schools only to be told that I had great qualifications but I needed some more "Canadian teaching experience." Someone recommended that I apply to be placed on the occasional teaching list, which would give me a chance to get a foot in the door of the profession.

As an occasional teacher, it does not allow me to realize my full potential but it gives me more insight into the schools' *modus operandi* as well as the semi-comforting feeling that I am almost there.

I can assure any other immigrant considering work as a teacher that it can be achieved but the journey is not an easy one. It takes lots and lots of determination, patience, tolerance, encouragement, and, most of all, faith to achieve such a goal, but it is possible.

Khaled Islaih: Using the Internet as a tool for newcomer settlement

As a Canadian newcomer, the Internet has facilitated my immigration and settlement significantly. I used the Internet before coming to Ontario to gather information about Canada and immigration regulations.

For example, I prepared for the immigration interview through Internet search. The information on the net (especially **www.settlement.org**) was very helpful for settlement research and preparation. I learned about the procedures to do the requested paper work upon arrival in Ontario. I learned how to open a bank account, enrol my children in school and apply for a Social Insurance Number, etc.

Moreover, Internet and email communications helped me initiate contacts with several Canadian professional organizations. For example, I joined the Professional Writers Association of Canada before arrival in Ontario. Today, the Internet has very useful and practical tips for immigrants to help them plan a successful settlement in their new country and stay connected with their country of origin through online newspapers, radio and TV channels.

A few months after arrival in Mississauga, my access to Internet from home helped me benefit from the online employment and learning opportunities. I am now contracted as a Google web analyst. I am doing my exciting and informative job from home. At the same time, I am enrolled in an intensive online career management professional program with Life Strategies of British Columbia.

Using the Internet for work and education purposes has eased my settlement in Mississauga significantly. More precisely, it helped me earn income to support my family, upgrade my skills to increase my employability in the Canadian job market and take care of family settlement issues on a daily basis.

All in all, the combination of the Internet, and positive thoughts and action is the key for my successful start in Canada. Therefore, I would like to invite new immigrants to use the Internet in their immigration and settlement. We are lucky in this country, because Canada is one of the leading countries in information and communication technologies. As new immigrants, we need to upgrade our skills and interests to access the existing opportunities in the e-world.

Sarvpreet G., chartered financial analyst

A dream to have a better life, desire to succeed along with a couple of professional qualifications, and some work experience was my baggage when I arrived in Canada almost four years ago.

I had done my research before coming to Canada about the relevance of my qualifications and the suitability to the current job market. The analysis concluded that the risk (moving to Canada) was worth the return (better lifestyle). A risk versus return statement made perfect sense as per my CFA (Chartered Financial Analyst) and MBA qualifications.

Being computer literate, I first went online and started applying for jobs hoping to get at least a couple of interviews. I did not get a single response. I decided to approach some of the employment agencies. I was out of luck again as I was focused on the industry of my choice – finance.

In order to supplement my previous education, I enrolled in the Canadian Securities Course (CSC), an industry recognized entry-level program for finance. However, I would like to clarify that the CSC was in no way an upgrade to my existing qualifications. The course content represented only about five per cent of my existing CFA qualification. But I had to do it as the CFA from India is not a recognized qualification.

After three weeks of frantic job search, visiting the Human Resources and Social Development Centres (HRSDC), and talking to a number of people, I realized that there was one big obstacle in my path to success – "no Canadian experience". My elder brother, who has been in Canada since 1998, suggested that I try the Voluntary Work Co-op Program offered by Dufferin-Peel Adult Education Centre. Running out of options, I decided to take a shot at this. I reluctantly joined their 19-week program (full time), which included eight weeks of classroom sessions followed by 11 weeks of voluntary job placement.

The job search was still on. During the eight weeks of class, I was convinced that I would have to start at an entry-level position. After several interviews, I finally tasted success – as a customer service representative with one of the major banks in Toronto. That was the golden chance (the proverbial foot in the door) I was waiting for. I knew it was going to be a long way to go to get to the position which reflects my qualifications and experience, but I was prepared for it.

My initial performance and discussions with my manager landed me a full-time opportunity as a financial services manager. My struggle to get a job ended after five months, but the struggle to get to the right position continues.

My advice to new immigrants is to stay focused on your goal. You may have to constantly change and manage your short-term objectives, but as long as you do not lose sight of the long-term objectives, dreams can become reality.

Hyacinth, channel manager

My first five months in Canada has taught me "the art of survival", though I know there are still a lot of lessons awaiting me and for which I know I have developed the art of survival. I came to this country with "big" dreams, but I have realized that things don't happen in a linear way as I had thought.

I thought being a qualified and experienced professional would make it fairly easy for me to get into the job market. So I immediately and aggressively started my job search by jumping straight into a government-funded program, attending job fairs, networking, registering with employment agencies, posting my résumé online, and cold calling.

I was positive that I would get a job, but I didn't know what was waiting for me down the road. The reality of the "Canadian experience" or lack thereof, became my roadblock. Suddenly my professional training, experience, and academic qualifications seemed not to be enough and the doors wouldn't open. I was thrown into shock when all that seemed available were entry-level positions. My brain rejected this and so I pushed back at the system refusing to accept it, until I realized that this strategy would get me nowhere, especially when I needed to pay the bills and put food on the table.

I reassessed my situation, and decided not to fight the system but to work with it. I got a part-time entry-level job within my industry within 10 days of applying. That was enough for now, because it would give me the "Canadian experience" while allowing me to pursue other opportunities. I started to focus on the bigger picture, because I knew this was only "part time" until I could earn enough to go "full time".

I decided to use Sun Tzu's concepts on **"The Art of War"** to help me, and I quote them below as I believe they are great for anyone who wants to win.

1. **Know Your Battlefield**. Get down to the basics and learn about the country and its culture. "Shut up and listen." Have an open mind, be flexible and learn what you need to know so you can make your important decisions.

2. **Thoroughly Assess Conditions**. Thoroughly assess the situation before making a decision in order to develop your spirit of mission.

3. **Be Flexible**. Winning isn't easy. Revise plans as you go along and make adjustments as required. Ensure you keep your eyes on the big picture at all times.

4. **Know Yourself; Know Your Opponent**. "Know your enemy and know yourself and you will never be defeated." The best way to gain this knowledge is go into the heart of your opponent's battlefield and work from within. You can't gain Canadian experience from the periphery. You have to go into the system to gain this knowledge and experience to overcome the obstacle.

5. **Win Without Fighting**. The best victory is the one where you don't have to fight. It is important that you seek victory before going out, otherwise you will have to fight with the hope of winning. Develop win-win strategies by researching, doing the right things, staying positive and decide no matter what the situation you would have learnt and benefited anyway. This will help you in achieving your goal.

(Reference for quotes: The Art of War for Managers: 50 Strategic Rules, by Gerald A. Michaelson, 2001 Published by Adams Media Corporation)

Aruni, accountant from Sri Lanka

I arrived in Canada in the fall of 1996, with more than eight years of experience in the field of accounting and finance, of which five years were spent as a financial analyst in the corporate planning department of a large group of companies, with more than 15 diverse subsidiaries operating under it.

Since accounting practices are generally the same all over the world, I expected to find employment in my related field, although I knew that initially I might not get the same position I held in my country of origin as there would be a learning curve due to cultural and industrial differences.

However, my initial job search proved frustrating due to most recruiting firms requiring Canadian experience as well as a Canadian qualification.

I fulfilled my requirement for Canadian qualification, by registering as a student with a Canadian accounting body, the Certified General Accountants (CGA) of Ontario. They evaluated my international qualifications and I received some credits, which enabled me to start at a higher level in their qualifying system, and therefore earn my CGA designation quicker.

Obtaining Canadian work experience, however, proved much harder. If Canadian work experience is a requirement prior to employment, how does one obtain this much valued experience if no prospective employer is willing to take a chance on the individual?

This is where networking within my own community helped. Members of my alumni who had migrated before me, kept their eyes and ears opened for me, and through their help I was able to obtain that much-needed first break into the Canadian workforce. A word of caution here, in that your first job may be at a much lower level than what you had previously held in your country of origin, but you need to take it and prove yourself and then slowly but surely you will be able to move up the corporate ladder.

In a nutshell, breaking into the Canadian workforce requires an individual to be able to deliver what the system requires – the related qualification and experience. This might entail night and/or weekend school as well as networking. Last but not least, be optimistic and have a positive attitude and this, together with hard work, will help you reach your career goal.

Muhammad, software engineer from Pakistan

I immigrated to Canada from the United States with lots of hope and confidence, and never thought it would've been difficult finding a job in Canada, as I had had international as well as North American work experience with Fortune 500 companies.

I found it hard to get a new job, with employers asking the same question "Do you have any Canadian work experience?" Aah!!! I went through so many interviews, and was desperate and discouraged at the same time, but I kept my hopes alive.

Finally I was introduced to a job-search program, which was quite useful. I learned some new ways to conduct my job search. I was able to make new friends and network, and we all encouraged each other, but the most important thing was that at the end of the program I had gained more confidence. The program gave me the hope and courage that I was losing at time.

Initially, I found some small contract work, but finally I landed a nice position with a well-known information technology company, which is a global leader in technological innovations. I faced many hardships in getting back into my career. I struggled, but the encouragement from others built my confidence and I kept working towards my goal. I really appreciate all those who helped me to achieve my goals.

I would encourage anyone in such a position not to get discouraged, hold their heads up and move forward; always working towards your goal and keeping hope alive.

Gurdip, professional engineer and businessman: Gaining Canadian Experience

I think there are two important aspects of your qualifications which help you in your career objectives. One is getting Canadian credentials for your profession and the other is to get involved in volunteer work.

I've been in Canada since 1975. I had to struggle a lot to get my first job in Canada. Even though I had an engineering degree from India, it wasn't easy to get a break on the employment front. The employers looked for Canadian experience or at least Canadian credentials before they would consider me.

I was convinced very quickly that the best way to get employment was to work towards getting the professional engineer's designation. Since that was going to take two or three years to accomplish, I needed some kind of employment to put food on the table. My engineering degree became an obstacle in getting a low-paying job because the employers thought I was overqualified for such jobs. Finally, I had to understate my qualifications to get a shipper/receiver's position for survival. I did get my professional engineering designation and an engineering position later.

I've also found that volunteer work may give you double rewards. It's food for your soul anyway and sometimes it helps in enhancing your career. In recognition of my professional background and my involvement in the community, I was appointed as Chairperson of the Employment Insurance Board of Referees in 1995. I served there for nine years.

Eduardo Fagioli from Argentina

I arrived in Canada in July 1987 from Argentina, with plans that my wife would join me as soon as I had secured employment and rented a place to live. A good friend of mine, who had lived in Canada for six years, oriented me to the Canadian way of life during those very stressful times.

I first enrolled in an ESL (English as Second Language) course to improve my language skills and began looking for employment in my field (information technology). After a month of not receiving any responses, I put aside my plans to work in my field and concentrated my efforts on securing some form of an income in order to bring my wife to Canada.

I took a part-time job delivering newspapers and continued my search for a full-time job. In addition to my degree in Operational Research from Buenos Aires, I had also the equivalent of a Mechanical Technologist certificate so I thought I could use those skills to find a job in manufacturing.

I was offered a job as a material handler in a heavy machinery factory in Mississauga, Ontario, working the night shift. I took the job because my English was very poor, but I kept reminding myself it was only for a short time.

My wife arrived in Canada in October 1987 and, one week later, I quit my newspaper delivery job and continued working in the factory on the day shift. Early in 1988, I applied for a stage material calculation and bill of material rationalization position in the engineering office, and was hired.

The company declared bankruptcy in late 1989 while I was away on vacation. In my desperation, I followed up on an interview I had done a couple of weeks before and the gentleman explained to me that the position was no longer available, but, because of my circumstances, he would see what he could do.

The following Monday, he called me for a second interview and I started working immediately as a production programmer and production coordinator for this business equipment manufacturing company. At the same time, I completed my degree in systems analysis from Buenos Aires.

In 1990, the same person who hired me at the business equipment company left the company and, shortly afterwards, he called me to tell me there was an opening for a programmer analyst position in the company. I was interviewed by the controller and the president, and was hired.

At the end of 1994, I was promoted to manager of information systems and gained a lot of experience. Four years later, I decided to use the services of a headhunter to begin a systematic job search again.

In May of the same year, I accepted the position of manager, information technology development with one of the largest medical laboratories in Ontario. This was a very challenging and enriching environment where I learned a lot and polished my managerial and leadership skills. But, after seven years, I was downsized.

Suddenly, I was jobless again and in urgent need to assess my financial situation. During this assessment process, two very important thoughts started to take shape in my mind:

The first was the realization that, after many years of good, honest and hard work I was unemployed and left to my own luck, and regaining employment at the same professional and salary level was going to be a difficult challenge. Secondly, the thought of self-employment came to mind and, with the help of my friend who is a financial planner, I decided to embrace a different challenge and shift to financial planning.

Today, I'm working my way to become a financial planner. I sincerely hope my story will be of help to you and show that commitment, persistence, honesty, and integrity are always rewarded, and that there are always special people who will appear in your life just at the time you need them most to offer assistance.

Jin, electrical engineer from China

After having worked for many years in some major engineering design institutes in China as an electrical engineer, I immigrated to Canada two years ago. During this time, I experienced the most difficult challenges in my life. Although I had visited North America many times before and I had done enough preparation before moving from China, I did not expect to meet with such difficulty.

After settling down, I began to plan my future. First, I made an appointment to take the test to obtain my driver's license. Within a month, I got it and this allowed me to go wherever I wanted. I then enrolled in a three-week job finding program, which gave me basic ideas about the Canadian job market: how to prepare résumés and cover letters according to Canadian standards, and how to find and get a job in a reasonable time. Once I finished that class, I began searching websites and newspapers for job postings, and after two weeks, I got my first job as an office clerk. I found this job four months after landing in Canada.

While working at this job, I still kept gathering information about professional jobs in the electrical field. My research led me to a non-profit organization that operates a Mentoring Program for internationally-educated engineers. I applied for this program and got an opportunity to talk with some professionals in an engineering consulting company. I received a job offer from this company to be an electrical designer the next day and started my professional career in Canada seven months after landing

Immigrating to a new country is hard, but preparation is necessary. The main barrier for me was my language skills, so you are advised to sharpen your skills if you plan to immigrate. After landing, enrol in some courses to help you get familiar with the community and the job market.

Work hard and keep upgrading your skills to be a qualified professional.

Kally, an electrical engineer from China

I immigrated to Canada from China in October 2002 for family reasons, and it took me four years to finally find a job in my field of electrical engineering.

When I arrived in Canada, I was really confused about starting over because I did not know English very well and that made me very depressed. I could not find a job in my field, so some friends suggested I change my profession to accounting because it was difficult for women to get into engineering. I decided to study business administration but first had to study very hard to improve my English. Once I enrolled at the college, I realized I did not want to change my career as an engineer. I had spent 14 years as an electrical engineer in China and I did not want to give up my profession. I decided I was never going to give up on studying and finding a job in my field. I went to one of the universities to upgrade my knowledge in electrical engineering.

In the meantime, I continued looking for work and, one day, I was visiting the resource center to look for an employment counsellor when the case manager recommended me to the Job Search Keys program. I learned how to write a good and effective résumé and cover letter, and improved my interview skills. After finishing this program, the case manager recommended me to the Job Mentoring Program at **S.U.C.C.E.S.S.** The coordinator taught participants how to prepare good and effective questions for the mentor; how to improve our communication and language skills, and how to revise our résumés to reflect our employment background. I was matched with a very good mentor, an electrical engineer. This individual has his P. Eng. (Professional Engineer) designation, a highly-valued qualification granted by the Professional Engineering Society of each province. He helped me to understand the electrical industry, revised my résumé to fit the electrical profession, and gave me and other job seekers an opportunity to practice and conduct presentations in his office.

When he thought we were ready to make presentations to groups, he arranged for some hiring authorities to listen to our presentations. We were introduced to managers and team leaders, and our résumés were given to them for review.

Finally, after all these efforts, three of us from my group who participated in the mentoring program got contract job opportunities with an electrical engineering company in British Columbia. I was very happy that I could finally start working in my field.

I wouldn't have found this opportunity without networking. The case manager knew the coordinator of the Job Mentoring Program at **S.U.C.C.E.S.S.** and that led me to this golden job opportunity. I believe anyone who participates in a Job Mentoring Program is better equipped for interviews and job opportunities.

I would like to advise new immigrants to:

- Set up a feasible goal and be tenacious in working towards that goal. Never give up although it may sometimes seem difficult.
- Improve your language skills as it is very important for you to communicate very well.
- Keep up to date on new developments in your profession.
- Network with people in your desired profession. This will help you to meet and get to know employers and they will get a chance to know you.
- Treasure every opportunity that the society, organizations and individuals offer to you.
- Try your best to work hard, and gain respect and honour.
- Always find a way to help other newcomers, make some positive contributions and give back to society.

Although the economy may play a part in whether or not you will be successful in your job search, networking, good communication skills and personal tenacity are very important to your success.

K.C. Chau, job mentoring program coordinator, S.U.C.C.E.S.S., Vancouver, British Columbia

I am also one of the thousands of professional immigrants who suffered a lot after landing in Canada. I am a chemical engineer and had been in the chemical industry for over 20 years prior to moving to Canada. I was the General Manager/Director of a German chemical manufacturing plant based in China.

I have been in Canada since mid 1997. I could not find a job in my field during my first two years here. I evaluated my transferable skills and decided to pursue a Certificate Course for Legal Assistants because of its close match with my LLB degree that I received from England. Based on that degree, I got some exemptions from the program and completed it in 18 months.

I was fortunate to have had savings and assets, so it was not a problem for me to take any type of job that provided a small income while giving me a chance to get some Canadian Experience.

After the certification, I was still unable to find a job in that field, as it appeared that the field was dominated by mostly women. My next move was to become a Life Insurance Broker for one of the major life insurance companies, but that did not work out, so after a year I found labour work at a supermarket. I did this for 6 months while taking a course for Counselling (Bilingual Employment Services Advisor) at S.U.C.C.E.S.S. (United Chinese Community Enrichment Services Society), a non-profit community group based in Vancouver, British Columbia. I wanted to help people who were going through the same circumstances as I was.

Completing the course did not mean I would automatically get a job with the organization, but I took the opportunity to volunteer for almost six months with a group to develop a new program – from curricula development to facilitation. I was finally hired by S.U.C.C.E.S.S. in September 2002 and it was because the people I worked with recognized my level of competence. I am now the coordinator for a Job Mentoring Program

Although this is not my original profession, I am happy with what I am doing. It's the satisfaction that I get from this job that drives me to work from 9:00 a.m. to 9:00 p.m. (Quite often I need to work on Saturdays as well without being paid for overtime hours). I do this because I know I am making a profound difference in the lives of new immigrants. The only threat to me is the lack of job security since I am employed on a yearly contract, and I don't know what will happen next year.

Success Stories of Proactive Clients

The following stories show three very determined individuals who followed the job search path that led to success. They did what every savvy job seeker should do. They researched companies and industries; networked with people in and outside their fields; made cold calls even though it was not an easy task, and spent time recalling their stories and practising their interview skills. They also remained confident in their abilities and, most of all, persevered even when the situation appeared bleak.

James, project coordinator, Construction

James contacted me after he had submitted his résumé to an employment agency in response to a job posting. He received an email from a staffing manager suggesting he should get a professional résumé done before he could put his name forward to the hiring company.

When James and I met, the first thing he said to me was "Daisy, I am lost!" James, by the way, is not a new immigrant, but as Canadian as the Maple Leaf, however, he was having job search pains just like any other job seeker. He had recently returned to Brampton after 14 years in another city. He became frustrated at his last job because his abilities were being suppressed, not utilized.

We worked together for less than four weeks. After an in-depth interview process, I asked him to recall everything he did on the job that had a positive impact on the profitability of the company and specifically asked that he reflected on his accomplishments as project manager. He found the exercise useful as it forced him to think of things that wouldn't have come naturally to him in a conversation. I also suggested that he complete the DISC Behavioural Profile, an assessment that gives an idea of how some people respond to problems or challenges, how they influence others to their point of view, how they respond to the pace of the environment, and how they respond to rules and procedures set by others.

Initially, he was focusing on one small part of the assessment results, which he thought was a negative. We discussed the report in its entirety and he agreed that there were many positive qualities, and that he did have some areas for improvement.

He picked up his résumé and cover letter from me one Monday and, the same day, set out to target companies that could use his skills. He selected about 20 companies from two yellow pages directories and called each one to get their fax number and the name of someone to whom he could send his cover letter and résumé. He personalized the electronic copy of the cover letter and modified it to suit each company. On Friday when he called the last company, the person told him someone else would call him back on Saturday. During the telephone interview, the man's comments were "I like what I am hearing, can you come for an interview on Tuesday?"

He went for the interview and was given four different assessments, one of which was the same DISC assessment I had given him. He was a bit nervous as he felt they were going to see the same results that he perceived to be negative. He went home and two days later he was offered the job. He has found his dream job of project coordinator for a company in the steel fabrication industry, with the opportunity to travel across Canada and eventually to China. Not bad for someone who was lost and didn't know where to begin with his job search!

Ganet, interior designer

Ganet is from Egypt and, for years, she could not find a job in her field as an interior designer except to volunteer with her church by doing all the decorating and stage setup for their festivals and children shows. She got depressed many times and wanted to return to her country, but she persevered. She knew there were things she needed to learn, so she attended ESL classes to improve her English and completed two computer courses (AutoCAD) as most jobs required her to be able to design with the computer. Her only "real" job was as a sales clerk in a jewellery store. It was not in her field but it helped in building her customer service skills.

It became apparent that, to get a job in her field, she had to be a member of the Association of Registered Interior Designers of Ontario (ARIDO). To qualify for membership, she had to complete an in-depth questionnaire about her education and projects she had done during her training as well as a list of her major on-the-job projects. In addition, she had to submit a portfolio of her work. That exercise took months to complete, but after submitting all that was required, she was finally accepted as an Intern member of the association. Although she felt she could've qualified for full membership after 16 years' experience in Egypt, she was glad to have passed that hurdle.

Ganet continued going to her job in the jewellery store each day, but she never gave up her goal of finding a job in her field. Recently, through networking, she met someone who works with one of Canada's major home renovation companies. He suggested she send in an application to the company. She went for several interviews. They were very impressed with her portfolio and her background and offered her a job as a designer in their kitchen and bath department. Below is her note:

> *I don't know how to thank you, really Daisy. You worked with me to develop my résumé and cover letter, prepared me for membership in ARIDO, and coached me the day before my interview. You helped me in so many areas that words can't express. I can't forget you. Thanks and God bless you.* - Ganet G. – Interior Designer

Hyacinth, business development specialist

Hyacinth, an MBA graduate and new immigrant became tired of her survival job as a sales associate in a telephone store. She decided to quit her job, determined to find one that was commensurate with her education, skills and experience.

She focussed on companies within her industry and started getting interviews that were challenging yet interesting. At one interview, she had to prepare a PowerPoint presentation and deliver it before a panel of three people. She did not get the job as they decided to go with someone from within the company, but she made such a good impression on the interviewers that she was number one on their list for any similar position in the future.

The lessons she learned from that interview prepared her very well for her current job. She had four interviews – the first with two directors and a human resources specialist; the second with the manager with whom she is now working, the third was with the director for Ontario operations, and the fourth was with the Vice President for Canada. She was also asked to complete several pre-employment assessments.

At the end of it all, she was hired as Business Development Specialist, a job that was in line with her abilities and educational background. Ironically, the same day she signed the contract for this job, another job offer arrived by courier from the company that had promised to keep her on top of their list. "It never rains, but it pours".

Views from Recruiters and HR Experts

Suzanne McFarlane, former diversity sourcing specialist, BMO Financial Group and Hewitt Associates

A Recruiter's Advice

When it comes to the recruitment process, there are some challenges that all applicants share, including structuring an effective résumé, and preparing for the telephone and in-person interview. Within these areas, however, there are certain challenges that speak directly to the foreign-trained professional as she/he attempts to find meaningful work in the Canadian marketplace.

These challenges don't need to be barriers to employment, but rather opportunities for awareness and preparedness on the part of the applicant. As a recruiter, I hope that the advice below may be helpful to applicants and give them some insight into effective job search.

- **Assessment and Accreditation**

  Education assessment is a fundamental part of any résumé review and makes up part of the *minimum* qualifications that recruiters are looking for in an application. Unfortunately, this area is often overlooked by foreign-trained professionals, some of whom have decided to approach job search without the use of an agency or employment resource centre, sources which typically provide this information.

  Candidates should bear in mind that it is not the recruiter's responsibility to ask for evidence of equivalent education requirements. It is the candidate's responsibility to provide this information with or within their résumé. With the possible exception of education that has been awarded in the United States or, to a lesser extent, Great Britain, the recruiter's assumption is never that education is equivalent to the Canadian requirement.

  Each candidate would do well to give themselves the advantage when submitting their résumé by adding a line under their education, citing the equivalency and the organization that has assessed this. This allows the recruiter a smooth review of the application and could save the applicant from being overlooked.

- **The Interview**

  As a mosaic, Canada houses a number of cultures, languages and styles of communication. At times, these different styles can come into conflict with the corporate world – particularly during recruitment.

Some things that candidates can keep in mind during an interview include:

- Taking an appropriate amount of time to answer questions. Although this can be difficult, particularly in cases where English is not the primary language, it should be kept in mind and practiced. Oftentimes, it isn't that a candidate doesn't understand the questions being asked, but rather the amount of time it takes to translate the English question into one's native tongue, and then translate the answer back into English.

  In many cases, a recruiter does not understand that this is the process taking place, and can mistakenly come to the conclusion that the candidate is simply slow. This accounts for many frustrations, both on the part of the recruiter and the candidate during interview. If necessary, assure your interviewer that you do in fact understand the question, particularly if you find you are taking a longer than average time to respond. Also, remember to practice, practice, practice!

- Be prepared for "behaviourally-focused interviews" (BFIs). The BFI is a form of interview that most candidates will come across with Canadian employers. The BFI asks very specific questions about your past experience and how your involvement in that experience helped in its resolution. These questions are often multi-layered (i.e., a three-part question) and look to past behaviour as an indication of potential future performance.

- Don't assume that a recruiter will be impressed by the post-secondary school that you've attended. Depending on the part of the world one is from, candidates may assume that the prestige of his/her university or college carries with them – this is most often not the case. Generally speaking, regardless of the school attended, all candidates will still have to prove themselves and compete with a variety of other candidates. Do not présumé that your schooling or your résumé will speak for itself – you will need to back it up with experiential evidence and effective communication skills in order to impress your recruiter.

- Take advantage of internships. Internships that offer foreign-trained professionals the opportunity to participate in the workforce provide candidates with invaluable Canadian experience – something that I'm sure many have found to be in demand with some employers. Internships not only offer hands-on skills and acclimatization to the Canadian workforce, but also have the added value of providing networking opportunities for participants.

Ms A. Gentles, HR manager: New Country – New Job Opportunity

For many new immigrants, that first job in Canada means starting over, and most times, in areas unrelated to their training and education, or starting at the bottom of the rung, if fortunate enough to be hired in a related field. Most come into that job after months, sometimes years, of searching, remaining optimistic and holding on to the dream that brought them here. Even for those who are able to fast track into corporate Canada, typically transferred in from global branches of a local company, there are adjustments to be made in order to be successful.

There are two major adjustments – first to the Canadian culture and second to the culture of the organization they have joined. To successfully adjust, one needs to be very observant and be willing to put aside old assumptions and be open to new standards. However, the key to breaking down barriers and creating personal career success is no different for the new immigrant than for any other employee, in general. The new immigrant must be highly focused on the following:

- Gain clarity on what is expected in the role and how your success will be measured
- Understand how the role fits into the overall goals of the function and the company
- Determine what is important to your manager
- Get integrated into the team – get to know them, allow them to get to know you
- Know the strategy of the company
- Learn the "language" of the corporation
- Build relationships up the organization to create a support team. It is true that who you know is often more important that what you know – the "what" can come later
- Seek out people who are in positions to which you aspire and ask them to be your mentor
- Seek out opportunities to take on additional responsibilities (especially if your skills are underutilized)
- Deliver value
- Take advantage of training and development opportunities
- Be confident; be visible

Create career goals and share them with those on your support team. Work diligently towards them, stay positive and be adaptable as changes occur, as they must in the corporate world.

Marc Belaiche, former recruiter and President of TorontoJobs.ca: Job Search Tips for New Canadians

You are new to the country. You have high expectations of what your successful experience back home can bring you, and you want to get working quickly and show how your skills can help Canadian companies.

The experts at TorontoJobs.ca have come up with a list of suggestions for your job search. Many of them have been stated already in this book but it's good to read them again from a former recruiter's perspective:

- **Post Your Résumé On-Line**
  Posting your résumé on a website like TorontoJobs.ca increases your chances of being found by recruiters. Recruiters search résumé databases by keyword, skills, location, etc., to find appropriate candidates.

- **Take a Position Where you are Overqualified**
  There are many advantages to doing so, including getting Canadian experience quickly, networking with others, showing what you can do, and avoiding having your résumé show a time gap in between jobs.

- **Work with an Employment Agency**
  Employment agencies can help in your job search, but don't rely exclusively on them. They may be able to help you, but it may be something for which you are overqualified or perhaps something temporary.

- **Network, Network, and Network!**
  Make a list of all your contacts and ask them for assistance – anyone can help you in your search. You may be surprised at how powerful your network can be.

- **Join Associations**
  Join or volunteer with a local chapter of a professional/trade association. There are associations available for almost every area of expertise.

- **Find a Mentor**
  There are some government programs that can match you up with a mentor. The main one in the Greater Toronto Area is The Mentoring Partnership. You may also ask someone you know to be your mentor to guide you in your search.

- **Ask for Informational Interviews**
  Try to make contact with people in your area of expertise to see if they will give you information on how to help in your job search.

- **Attend Career Fairs**
  There are many career fairs in Toronto, including the New Canadian Job Fair. Going to a career fair can be very informative to help you in your job search, but don't expect to get a job at the fair itself. Bring many résumés and business cards.

- **Upgrade Your Skills/Education**
  There are many schools, colleges and other educational institutions that offer courses to upgrade your skills and/or knowledge on Canadian practices.

- **Get Your International Credentials Evaluated**
  Getting your international credentials evaluated to determine your equivalent standing in Canada can be very useful.

- **Take a Temporary Position**
  Similar to the advantages of taking a position that you are overqualified for, as described above, this option can get you some valuable experience and earn money to pay for on-going bills.

- **Follow-up on Interviews**
  Follow-up interviews with a thank-you note and touch base periodically with interviewers to see if any opportunities have come up, even if you didn't get the original position you applied for.

- **Start Your Own Business**
  If you are unable to find a satisfying job, starting your own business may be a worthwhile option. Think of what you are good at then conduct research around those skills or topics. Canada offers many opportunities for entrepreneurs and there is a high success rate among immigrants starting their own businesses.

- **Reward Yourself**
  Reward yourself when you have accomplishments in your job search. Try not to get discouraged – maintain a positive attitude. If you follow some or all of the suggestions above, you will certainly hear about opportunities.

Frances Vancer, president of HR Concepts

Over the years in human resources, I have interviewed many internationally-trained professionals. The first piece of advice I would give is to get your professional credentials assessed before you begin looking for a job.

The next important step is to take a serious look at your résumé to see if it's customized to the Canadian job market. To help with this process, you should visit a professional career counsellor or one of the many government agencies that provide job search assistance. These individuals or groups will help you rewrite your résumé to bring out the relevance of your international experience to the Canadian workplace. By using any of these services, you will be able to integrate at a faster rate. You should also find a professional association in your industry to enable you to begin to develop your network of contacts.

The third step is to find a mentor: someone who can give you a positive and realistic outlook on what needs to be done to adapt to the workplace, i.e., language skills, what it takes to get the job done, having a positive attitude, working on self-directed teams, and how to fit in.

While the above advice pertains to internationally-trained professionals, I also believe that professional associations should develop a program that will fast track these individuals to enable them to gain employment in their fields. Such an initiative will go a long way in alleviating the skills shortage that Canada faces.

We also have to be realistic! An engineer in Europe is required to spend more time in university than in Canada and, even with the lack of Canadian experience, that individual can design, build, and learn Canadian standards much quicker, because of his or her training. Similarly, it would not take a human resources professional who has recruited in his or her particular country for an international company very long to learn the Employment Standards and employment law requirements in Canada.

Finally, companies need to do their part by opening their doors to these professionals who are eager to contribute their skills and experience. Many volunteer their time through internship programs and, by so doing, have got the proverbial "foot in the door," but much more needs to be done. The shortage of talent that is on Canada's doorstep means organizations will have to review their hiring practices to include hiring internationally-trained professionals to fill the skills gap.

SECTION III

THE CANADIAN PERSPECTIVE

CHAPTER 11

Canadian Workplace Culture, Values and Expectations

"To know the road ahead, ask those coming back" – ***Chinese Proverb***

We all have our customs and values that we take from our respective countries and cultures. These sometimes create misunderstandings and confusion among the people we interact with on a daily basis. This section will give you an overview of Canadian culture and assist you in successfully integrating in the Canadian workplace. You will discover, however, during your daily interactions with your coworkers there are more similarities than differences among the group.

It is easy for us to relate to people from our own culture and background because we understand each other. It becomes a bit more difficult when we have to interact with people from other cultures because we might not understand or share the same values. Be very careful that your own biases don't cause you to expect certain behaviours from people because of their ethnicity, age, colour or gender.

While some of these values may have been covered in other sections of this book, it's well worth repeating here.

Expectations in the Workplace

- **Corporate Culture**
  Whether in an interview or in a general conversation, you may hear about corporate "culture" or corporate "fit". This is an indication that the person is looking to see if, and how well, you will fit into the company. You may have the required expertise, but most companies place a high value on people with "soft skills" – those who are ambitious, hard-working, positive, respectful, efficient, reliable, punctual, and honest. This means, that technical expertise is not all that is required to obtain a job – your attitude and attributes are also important.

- **Greetings and Introductions**
  When you are introduced to someone, shake their hands firmly and briskly. Look the person in the eye and smile. Unlike many cultures, in North America if you do not make eye contact with the person to whom you are speaking, you may give the wrong impression that you cannot be trusted. It could also be considered rude if you avoid looking at the person.

- **Communication Skills**

  As reported in the "Canada Labour Business Centre Immigration Handbook", a sizeable number (29 per cent) of new immigrants to Canada do not have language capability in either of the two official languages (English and French). As a result, many immigrants seek language training to upgrade their skills and improve their employment prospects (**www.clbc.ca/files/Reports/Immigration_Handbook.pdf**).

  It is usually understood that English is the language of international business. It's an asset to have the ability to speak several languages because of the growing diversity of the larger metropolitan areas of the country, but many job postings require candidates to be able to read, write and speak English. Others may specifically ask for bilingualism (English and French). If you settle in the Greater Toronto Area, fluency in English is a requirement. If you settle in Quebec, French is required.

  The fact that it is important to learn the official languages well does not mean that you have to downplay the relevance or value of your first language. In a country where many of us are still monolingual, your knowledge of other languages could be considered an asset. The multicultural makeup of urban centres like Toronto, Montreal and Vancouver makes knowledge of a second or third language an asset, so make your fluency in another language work for you.

- **Punctuality**
  Canadian time means what the clock says! Punctuality is highly valued in both business and social settings. If you have been told to arrive at 9 a.m., make sure you are on time. It's even better if you arrive about 10 minutes early, particularly for an interview.

- **Respect**
  Treat everyone you meet with the same courtesy and respect. Sometimes how you treat the receptionist, the security guard or the administrative assistant at a company may determine whether or not you get the job. Many HR people make it a point to ask the person at the front desk for their opinion on candidates, so be on your best behaviour with everyone.

  Although you may be tired and feel ruffled at the end of the interview, maintain your professionalism right to the end. On leaving, make sure your posture shows the same confidence and energy you had at the beginning. Shake hands again and be sure to thank the interviewer for his or her time.

- **Harassment in the Workplace**
  Harassment refers to unwelcome comments or actions that make a person feel uncomfortable and humiliated. The Ontario Human Rights Code, (Subsection 5(2) states:

Every person who is an employee has a right to freedom from harassment in the workplace by the employer or agent of the employer or by another employee because of race, ancestry, place of origin, colour, ethnic origin, citizenship, creed, age, record of offences, marital status, same-sex partnership status, family status or disability.

There are two very common forms of harassment that you should be aware of – **Sexual** and **Racial**.

Sexual harassment is any unwanted attention and can include touching, comments of a sexual nature or anything degrading. A young man who immigrated to Canada thought it was okay to put his arm around the shoulders of one of his female co-workers as they walked from lunch. She reported the incident to the human resources department and he was escorted out of the building later that day. It was a culture shock to him as in his former country it was customary to hug a co-worker (or anyone for that matter) without it being called sexual harassment. It was such an embarrassing situation for him that he contemplated returning to his homeland.

Racial harassment is any comment, joke or action that puts down or embarrasses another person because of his or her race. Sometimes remarks are made innocently, but it can be interpreted differently by the other person.

- **Non-verbal (Body) Language**
Body language experts say that when we are communicating face-to-face, seven per cent is based on what we say and 93 per cent is based on our non-verbal communication – our attitude and appearance. When broken down further, 55 per cent is based on what people see and 38 per cent is based on our tone of voice. When we are communicating through the telephone, 70 per cent is based on our tone of voice while 30 per cent is based on our words.

These are very important statistics to keep in mind when we meet people, and contrary to the saying "never judge a book by its cover," it doesn't work that way all the time. We are judged by "our covers" long before we get an opportunity to confirm or disprove people's first impressions. Therefore, in preparing for interviews or other meetings, make sure you have a good understanding of what your body language is saying.

Facial Expression: Every now and again, take a look in the mirror to see the expression on your face while you are relaxing. Are you happy with your appearance? Is your face smiling back at you? An interviewer will be looking in your face to see your reaction and response to questions. Even if you mask your answer, your face will still show it. Put on a genuine smile. There's a popular quote that reads "a smile is a curve that keeps things straight." You want to keep things straight during and after the interview.

Eye Contact: Are you in the habit of looking the other way when speaking with people? In some cultures it is considered rude to look a person in authority in the face. However, in North America, it's different. If you want to score points with the interviewer, make sure you maintain eye contact. This shows them that you are confident and honest, and that you have nothing to hide. Maintaining eye contact does not mean you should stare at the individual either, because that may lead them to believe that you are hostile.

Handshake: In business, the official way to greet people in Canada is with a handshake. How is yours? Is it firm, and does it convey confidence and respect? Or, is it limp like wet noodles, or hard like a knuckle cracker? No one wants to shake hands with someone who barely offers the tips of the fingers or someone attempting to crush the finger bones.

In some cultures, it is customary that men do not shake hands with women. This does not apply in Canada as women have an equal role in the society. This means it is natural, in a formal business setting, for you to shake the hand of your interviewer, manager, supervisor or co-worker, whether male or female.

Seating: Never take a seat until you are invited to do so. Once seated, make sure to sit upright, but in a relaxed manner. Do not slouch nor sit on the edge of the chair. This will give the impression that you are nervous and lack confidence.

Hand Gestures: "Watch your hands, watch your hands, where they go!" That may be a catchy phrase from kindergarten, but it is quite applicable in the world of business. Sit with your hands in your lap to appear calm and confident, but never cross them in front of your chest. This gives the impression that you are distant, cold and defensive. It's all right to use hand gestures to help bring your point across, as long as it is not distracting and aggressive.

Feet and Legs: Place them flat on the floor. If you have to cross your legs, do so at the ankles under the desk where no one will see. If you sit with your ankle on your knee you will appear too casual and this could hurt your chances in the interview.

- **Dress Code**

As we have stated before, first impression counts and the way you are dressed sends a strong signal to people. According to image experts, 55 per cent of another person's perception of you is based on how you look. While many companies support a "business casual" dress code, it's vitally important that you make an effort to look polished and professional.

It is said one should always dress for the job one aspires for. Men will always look good in a tailored suit or a nice shirt and slacks, but because women's fashions are more diverse, they should pay attention to what they wear and how it's worn.

A navy blue suit was considered industry standard, but now image consultants have added a black suit to the list. No matter what you wear, clothes should be neat and clean, and shoes nicely polished. Women should forget dangly earrings and men shouldn't wear head gear inside a building, unless it's a fundamental part of their culture. Here is a suggested dress code checklist for both genders:

Women
- ✓ Solid colour, conservative suit
- ✓ Coordinated blouse
- ✓ Limited jewellery
- ✓ Moderate Shoes
- ✓ Neat, professional hairstyle
- ✓ Sparse make-up & perfume
- ✓ Manicured nails
- ✓ Hosiery/nylons/stockings) that fit your skin tone

Men
- ✓ Solid colour, conservative suit
- ✓ White long sleeve short
- ✓ Very limited jewellery
- ✓ Dark socks, professional shoes
- ✓ Neat, professional hairstyle
- ✓ Go easy on the aftershave
- ✓ Neatly trimmed nails
- ✓ Conservative tie

If you are not sure about the dress code of the company you're interviewing with, don't be afraid to stand around the parking lot or in front of the building to see what employees are wearing.

Clear Speech and Language Training
By Heather Chetwynd

One of the major barriers for many newcomers to Canada is language – the ability to converse fluently and clearly in one or both of Canada's two official languages – French and English. While having the ability to speak several languages can definitely be an asset given the growing diversity of the larger metropolitan areas of the country, most jobs require candidates to read, write and speak the primary language of the province.

Quebec residents require French but most of Canada is English-speaking. Refining your skills in English – being able to speak clearly, correctly and concisely – can be key to achieving success in the Canadian workplace.

When prospective employers ask about "Canadian experience", I believe they have two primary concerns: 1) that you know Canadian cultural norms and 2) that your language skills are good enough for comfortable, effective communication.

Understanding the culture, being familiar with the topic and concepts being discussed, knowing the idioms and vocabulary being used, speaking with an accent that the majority of people can easily understand – all these aspects will increase the ease with which communication takes place.

If we have to struggle to understand each other, it is uncomfortable and ineffective. As a result, if you can familiarize yourself with Canadian cultural behaviour, improve your English skills and refine the clarity of your speech, you will greatly increase your chances of obtaining the job you desire.

Language Training

If English is not your first language, make sure to enrol in a language training course. English language training is provided free or at a nominal cost in programs run by the school boards, of which there are two – the public system and the Catholic schools, which are open to people of all religions. Many community centres offer training either through the school boards or independently. As well, many post-secondary institutions have classes, some of which are free. And there are many private language schools also.

In addition, read the newspapers, watch television and listen to the radio. Visit the libraries where resources such as tapes, videos, and books are available to help you learn quickly and easily. Encourage those in your communities who have been in Canada for a longer period to speak with you in English (or French) to enable you to become fluent. Advanced newcomers may also consider one-on-one training offered primarily by private institutions.

All language training for non-native speakers of English is considered to be ESL - English as a Second (or third or fourth) Language. In Canada, there are a variety of these programs. Here are a few:

- **Language Instruction for Newcomers to Canada (LINC)** is a national program which is also offered overseas and is intended for immigrants and refugees only. Those with Canadian citizenship are not able to attend.

- **Enhanced Language Training (ELT)** is geared toward students with a high proficiency in English (Canadian Linguistic Benchmarks – CLB 7-10) who are looking for work. These programs help students to become job-ready by focusing on business language, Canadian culture, legal rights, job search, interview skills, etc., and generally have some type of job placement and/or mentorship included.

- **Occupational Specific Language Training (OSLT)** focuses on language required in specific professions and often includes cultural information so that the student will understand Canadian workplace culture.

For the most up to date and detailed information on language training, visit **www.settlement.org**.

Pronunciation and Clear Speech

All of us have an accent, which is derived from where we were born and raised. In Canada, there is a predominant accent, although you will find regional variations depending on where you travel. If your accent is very different from the mainstream accent, people will often find it difficult to understand you, even if you have been speaking English all your life. And if it is difficult to understand your pronunciation, people may tend to lose interest, get frustrated, misunderstand and, unfortunately, misjudge you.

So how can you make it easier for people to understand your speech? Here are a few tips:

- **Speak slowly.** This is the best way to clarify your speech. Often this simple change will help people better understand what you are saying. It gives them time to process what they hear and you have more time to make the sounds clearly.

- **Move your mouth and lips a lot during speech.** If you really exaggerate during practice, when you speak in a real situation, you will feel more comfortable with a wider range of movement. Watch yourself in a mirror; it should look comfortable although it may feel uncomfortable since you may not be used to it.

- **Keep some space between your teeth.** Most native English speakers in Canada tend to keep their teeth slightly apart. This brings the sound forward and makes it clearer. Many other English accents and second-language accents hold the sound further back in the mouth which creates a muffled sound to Canadians.

- **Watch people's faces** to see if they understand what you've said. You may need to repeat what you said or use different words in order for the meaning to be clear. If the person is looking at you when you speak, it will be easier to understand you. Also, face-to-face verses side-by-side communication makes hearing each other much easier. You may also ask them if they understand what you are saying.

- **Watch how you stress words and intonation**. Stress refers to the emphasis we put on words and parts of words. Intonation is the up and down melody of the voice. Make sure you learn correct syllable stress and practice exaggerating it. And learn which words we stress in sentences – generally all nouns, verbs, adjectives and adverbs. Intonation also carries a lot of meaning. Copy people to internalize common intonation patterns. Watch "up-talk" – many people raise their voice at the end of every sentence.

- **Learn how to pronounce the individual sounds** and make sure you pronounce the endings of words. Although Native speakers may drop endings, there are subtle ways we make the sounds understood. It is usually easiest for non-Native speakers to clearly make all the sounds normally pronounced. Use internet resources as references, such as **www.uiowa.edu/%7Eacadtech/phonetics/about.html#**, which shows how each sound is made, or the variety of online audio dictionaries.

- **Take every opportunity to speak with people in English** or **French**. Get over any fear you may have of making mistakes because most people do and you will too.

- **Read out loud**. When you see, say, and hear the words, your memory is reinforced and you have time to pronounce clearly. Use audio books or any audio recordings with transcripts and model the narrator if you like how he or she speaks.

- **Record yourself** during regular household conversations and while talking on the phone or reading aloud. Listen to the recording to see if you understood everything. If not, identify what the problem is and practice correcting it.

- **Repeat, Repeat, Repeat**. Repeat the speech of someone who has good enunciation. Choose a radio announcer you like. CBC (99.1 FM) has many and their speech is generally varied and clear.

Express Yourself Clearly

Culture is reflected in many aspects of behaviour, one of which is in how we interact with each other. In this regard, there are a few points worth mentioning. Of note, there are two aspects of Canadian culture which affect how we address each other.

One is that we are "egalitarian" as opposed to "hierchical". This means we have little tolerance for special treatment due to status and like to think of everyone as equal, which tends to result in more informality.

Our preference for informality means we often call each other by their first names. It is common for employees to be on a first-name basis with their employers. However, this is not always the case so, if you are unsure, use their title and last name and then let them tell you what they prefer.

We generally limit ourselves to using the titles Dr., Mr., Mrs. and Ms. (the neutral term for women) as Mrs. refers only to a married woman. Don't assume an older woman is married or that a married woman wants to be referred to as such. In general, following how other people address each other is a safe choice. Note: customer service agents tend to ask if they can call the client by their first name.

The second cultural aspect which influences how we communicate is related to living in a multicultural society. This has created what is called a "low-context" culture. This means that what may be understood in a less diverse culture with fewer words needs to be made explicit, given the fact that people hold such diverse values and beliefs and may misinterpret each other more easily. So we tend to be explicit, yet polite.

Our politeness is expressed in many ways. One is through small talk, which may seem unimportant, but it is how we develop and maintain relationships. Co-workers generally greet each other by asking "How are you?" "How is your day going?" "Did you have a nice weekend?" They are not trying to pry nor do they want a detailed explanation. A simple "I am fine, thanks" or "I had a nice weekend, thank you" is enough. But they also expect that you would respond by asking them a similar question.

Another way we express politeness is by softening our communication so as not to offend each other. Canadians are famous for saying "sorry". Even if someone bumps into you, it is normal to apologize. When it comes to giving delicate feedback, including any criticism, soften it by using suggestions, conditionals (could, would) and vocabulary that is not harsh. For example, if you want to say "This work is bad," you might say "This work could use some improvement" or "Perhaps you could re-do this part." Don't assume that such softness isn't serious. And be careful not to be too rough when giving feedback. People will think you are rude.

Expressing yourself well can take some time to learn. Make a point of observing people and modeling your language after theirs. And remember, communication is influenced to a very large degree by your body language. If you smile a lot - another Canadian habit - and show consideration, people will respond to your friendliness and forgive many language imperfections.

One Hundred Most Common English Expressions (Idioms)

Scattered throughout this book are some common phrases or expressions that you will hear from time to time as you interact with people at business and social events, and as you engage in small talk. Many of these are expressions Canadians take for granted and while you may be familiar with some of them, they form such an important part of our everyday conversations that the original list of 25 were not enough. With the help of UseofEnglish.com, the list was extended and appears below:.

- **Ahead of the pack/Ahead of the game** – ahead of the others; leading

- **All ears** – listening attentively

- **All set** – ready

- **At the drop of a hat** – immediately or quickly

- **Baby boomer generation** – anyone born between 1945 and 1967

- **Back burner** – not treated as a priority

- **Back to square one** – starting all over

- **Bean counter** – usually refers to an accountant

- **Beat around the bush** – not saying something clearly or taking a long time to say

- **Bend over backwards** – someone will do everything to help

- **Beside the point** – not related to the topic of the discussion

- **Beyond the shadow of a doubt** – sure or certain

- **Bite off more than you can chew** – take on too much responsibility and unable to handle it all

- **Bite the bullet** – face the situation although it may difficult and unpleasant

- **Blow (or toot) your own horn** – boasting, bragging when overdone or, with modesty, speaking about your accomplishments

- **Bottom-line** – profit; the financial status of the company. You may be asked "what contribution can you make to the company's bottom-line "profitability?"

- **Bureaucratic red tape** – has a negative meaning, which is usually associated with how long it takes to get government services or approvals

- **Butterflies in your stomach** – feeling nervous before an interview, for example

- **Call the shots** – the person in charge who makes decisions

---

- **Caught between a rock and a hard place** – in a situation where whichever option is taken it is going to be a difficult one
- **Change of heart** – change the way you think or feel
- **Cold shoulder** – ignoring someone
- **Comfort zone** – a place (or feeling) where one is relaxed and comfortable
- **Cut to the chase** – get to the point; say what needs to be said
- **Cutting or leading edge** – at the forefront of change
- **Don't judge a book by its cover** – do not judge someone or something by appearances; there is more to that person than what's on the outside.
- **Drag your feet** – taking too long to do something you really don't want to do
- **Draw the line** – making up your mind how far you will go and what you will accept
- **Eleventh hour** – at the last minute
- **Finding a needle in a hay stack** - trying to find or do something that is very difficult or impossible
- **Fine tuning** – doing last minute adjustments to make sure everything is working well
- **Fish out of water** – lonely or lost; maladjusted
- **Fit the bill** – it is perfect; it is what is necessary to do the task
- **Food for thought** – something for you to think about
- **Foot in the door** – an opportunity; a start
- **Foot the bill** - responsible for paying the bill
- **From the horse's mouth** – coming directly from the person concerned or responsible
- **Game plan** – a strategy: a methodical way to get achieve a goal
- **Gatekeepers** – people who control access to opportunities or to other individuals
- **Give and take** – compromise
- **Glass ceiling** – when people are not promoted in companies even though they are qualified – mostly applied to women in managerial positions
- **Heads will roll** – if something goes wrong, someone will be punished for it
- **High and dry** – left alone; abandoned without getting help when you need it
- **Hit the ground running** – prepared and ready to make a contribution

- **Hit the nail on the head** – you are correct or you said the right thing
- **Hit the sack** – you are ready to go to bed
- **Hold the fort** – you are in charge while the other person is away
- **In a jam** – someone is in a difficult situation or is in trouble
- **In a nutshell** – a quick summary
- **It costs an arm and a leg** – it's very expensive
- **Jane or John Doe** – a man or woman whose name is kept a secret or who is unidentified
- **Jump on the bandwagon** – joining with others to support a cause or event that is currently very popular, for example, the fight against HIV/AIDS
- **Jury's out** – can't come to a decision or an agreement on something
- **Keep abreast/Keep posted/Kept in the loop** – keep up to date and informed
- **Keep your chin up** – be confident; everything will work out fine
- **Keep your fingers crossed** – waiting to hear some good news
- **Knows the ropes** – has experience; knows how to get things done
- **Left in the dark** – excluded; not given any information
- **Level playing field** – everyone is treated equally
- **Light at the end of the tunnel** – although things are difficult at the moment, there is hope that things will get better soon
- **Lower your sights** – you accept something that is less than you had hoped. For example, you decide to take a survival job because it's difficult to find the one you really want
- **Make hay while the sun shines/Strike while the iron is hot** – take advantage of a good situation as it may not last
- **Melting pot / Multiculturalism** – an environment that fosters the acceptance and integration of people from diverse ethnic groups
- **Mind your P's and Q's** – be on your best behaviour
- **Miss the boat** – too late for an opportunity
- **Mover and shaker** – a person with influence. For example, the movers and shakers of Bay Street who help to shape economic policies.
- **My hands are full** – you have a lot of responsibility and you cannot accept anything else
- **My hands are tied** – I am unable to do anything to help
- **Not my cup of tea** – something that you do not like

- **Number cruncher** – someone who is good with numbers and pays attention to all the financial details
- **Off the cuff** – doing something without preparation, for example, giving an impromptu speech at Toastmasters
- **On the ball** – well-informed; knowledgeable
- **On the house** – free. The drink at the restaurant is on the house – it is free.
- **On the same page** – in agreement
- **Pain in the neck** – a very annoying and bothersome person
- **Pass the buck** –passing on responsibility to someone else
- **Powers that be** – decision-makers; those who are in charge
- **Push the envelope** – to go to the limit; to do something or take a situation outside the normal realm
- **Rat race** – a very competitive environment, usually associated with work
- **Rack your brain** – to think very hard or to try and remember something
- **Red carpet** – brought out for someone who is considered to be very important and therefore deserves special treatment
- **Reinvent the wheel** – redoing what has already been done before
- **Rome was not built in day** – it takes time for things to happen
- **Ruffle a few feathers** – saying or doing something that is unpopular; a decision to make changes or improvements that annoy or upset others
- **Run the show** – in control of the situation
- **Skeleton in the closet** – a shameful secret that someone does not want to reveal
- **Slap on the wrist** – little or no punishment for doing something wrong
- **Status quo** – a situation that remains the same; no change
- **Step up to the plate** – being brave and taking on the responsibility
- **Taken for a ride** - being deceived by someone
- **The ball's in your court** – the decision is up to you
- **Think out of the box** – stretch your imagination; be creative
- **Throw in the towel** – to give up
- **Too many irons in the fire** – too many projects going on at the same time; multitasking

- **Vicious circle/Vicious cycle** – a sequence of events that make each other worse – someone drinks because they are unhappy at work, then loses their job, and they drink more

- **Up in the air** – no decision has been made up to that point

- **Up and running** – ready to perform

- **Up to speed** – giving a summary of what has been happening

- **Wake-up call** – an experience that causes you to take stock of a situation and reflect on an action

- **Walk a mile in someone's shoes** - try to understand someone instead of criticizing them

*(Permission granted by UseofEnglish.com (**www.useofenglish.com**) to use a number of these expressions.)*

CHAPTER 12

The Canadian Labour Market

Learning about the Canadian labour market is a very important part of your job search. You will want to know and understand:

- where the job vacancies are
- what qualifications are required
- what salaries are paid for the different positions
- what sector is hiring or laying off
- what's happening locally, regionally and nationally

When you become knowledgeable about the labour market, it helps you to make informed decisions on where to find jobs, and probably where you want to live. As a new immigrant, it makes sense to consider employment options in the areas where there is demand for workers. Sometimes this may mean moving to another region or province.

Canadian Occupational Projection System

Human Resources and Skills Development Canada (HRSDC) develops projections of future labour demand and labour supply by broad skill level and by occupation, using the models of the Canadian Occupational Projection System (COPS). These projections allow for identifying those occupations that are likely to face shortage or surplus of workers over the medium term. Additional information can be found at **www.workingincanada.gc.ca/**.

The Labour Market Information Service:

- provides detailed labour market information at the local or community level
- analyses data and local events in order to identify community specific labour market trends and opportunities
- works with other labour market players, including businesses, educational institutions and local and provincial governments
- ensures people have access to quality labour market information.

Source: **www.labourmarketinformation.ca**

A very good resource, particularly for career practitioners, is the book "Making Sense of Labour Market Information". It introduces career practitioners to key socio-economic and labour market concepts, trends and issues. It also provides practical examples for researching labour market information and using that information in the career development process.

Source: **www.makingsense.org**.

Regulated and Non-regulated Occupations

Some occupations such as veterinarian, electrician, plumber, physiotherapist, medical doctor, engineer, among others, are called "regulated occupations". This is to ensure that professionals meet the required standards of practice and competence, and acts as a safeguard against unscrupulous practitioners. Approximately 20 percent of Canadians fall into this category.

- *Regulated Occupations*
  A "regulated" occupation is usually controlled by provincial, territorial and sometimes federal law and governed by a professional organization or regulatory body. The regulatory body sets entry requirements and standards of practice; assesses applicants' qualifications and credentials, and determines whether to certify, register or license qualified applicants.

  Such organizations also have the authority to discipline members of the profession/trade. There are specific requirements for entry, which may vary from one province to another. If you require additional information, it's best to check with the organization that represents your occupation. Note that some occupations are regulated in certain provinces and territories and not regulated in others.

  One of the well-known regulatory organizations is the Canadian Council of Professional Engineers (CCPE) which has extensive experience in evaluating foreign engineering credentials. The Engineering International-Education Assessment Program (EIEAP), the evaluation arm of CCPE, assesses the educational qualifications of individuals who were trained outside of Canada, by comparing their education to a Canadian engineering education. The EIEAP, according to their website, is the only assessment service in Canada specializing *exclusively in the assessment of engineering education credentials.*

- *Non-Regulated Occupations*
  The majority of occupations fall in the "non-regulated" category for which there is no legal requirement or restriction on practice with regard to licenses, certificates or registration.

Credential Assessments

Many immigrants to Canada arrive with impressive credentials. However, the training and certification that contributed to the points necessary to enter the country are often rejected in the employment line. Given the number of immigrants entering Canada and the incredible diversity of countries in which certification was obtained, the problem of credential recognition, the need for assessment services and flexibility of licensing bodies has never been greater.

Many of today's occupations require certification from a recognized educational institution, professional association or governing body. A recent survey by Statistics Canada illustrates the painful progress made by skilled immigrants seeking recognition for credentials earned outside Canada. – **Immigration and Skills Shortages – Canada Labour and Business Centre (CLBC)**

As the above quote suggests, many employers and hiring managers do not understand how to assess or compare the education of someone trained outside of Canada with those educated within Canada. As such, it is advisable that before you arrive or as soon as you arrive you get your educational qualifications assessed to determine their equivalency to Canada's academic standards. This gives you and potential employers an idea of how your qualification compares with the Canadian standard. There are several agencies and institutions that offer assessment services for a fee.

Assessment organizations fall into two groups – those that are provincially mandated and those that follow the "Guiding Principles for Assessment Practice" as directed by the Canadian Information Centre for International Credentials (CICIC).

- **The Canadian Information Centre for International Credentials**
  As noted on its website, the Canadian Information Centre for International Credentials (CICIC) "collects, organizes, and distributes information, and acts as a national clearing house and referral service to support the recognition and portability of Canadian and international educational and occupational qualifications".

  CICIC advises individuals, in Canada's official languages (English and French), on what they need to do to have their credentials assessed and recognized in Canada, and refers them to appropriate institutions and organizations for specific assistance. CICIC does not grant equivalencies or assess credentials, nor does it intervene on behalf of applicants or participate in appeals (**www.cicic.ca**).

  While most provinces have their own credential assessment agencies, which are able to assist individuals inside and outside of Canada, the major ones in Ontario are:

  - Comparative Education Service (University of Toronto)
  - World Education Service
  - International Credential Assessment Service of Canada

- **Comparative Education Service** (University of Toronto)
  The University of Toronto's Comparative Education Service (**www.adm.utoronto.ca/ces/#A**) has been providing professional academic assessments since the 1960s. The service evaluates non-

Canadian academic qualifications and equates them to Canadian qualifications which may be used for employment and immigration purposes.

- **World Education Services** (WES)
  WES converts educational credentials from any country in the world into their Canadian equivalents. It describes and validates each certificate, diploma or degree earned and states its academic equivalency in Canada.

  Nancy Millard of WES says that a credential evaluation by WES helps to determine the authenticity of documents, the status of institutions that issue them and the appropriate Canadian equivalency. WES understands the difficulty employers face in interpreting the vast array of credentials issued by institutions worldwide as well as the frustration of internationally-educated immigrants who cannot find employment.

  With over 30 years experience in evaluating international academic credentials and providing North American equivalences, WES has built up a database of over 40,000 institutions from more than 200 countries, and provides about 60,000 evaluation reports every year.

- **International Credential Assessment Service of Canada** (ICAS)
  The ICAS provides credential assessment services through its offices across Ontario. The information provided helps individuals achieve personal, career and educational goals; and helps employers, educational institutions, immigration authorities, community agencies, and other organizations to understand international credentials.

CHAPTER 13

Basic Requirements for Newcomers

While this book is primarily a career survival guide, one cannot conduct an effective job search if certain basic conditions are not met. This section of the book is designed to give you basic information as it relates to banking, applying for your social and health insurance cards, obtaining a driver's license, finding a family doctor, registering your children in schools, etc.

Banking and Credit

"Borrowing from your future for a nice life today provides only temporary comfort. When the bills are due, the stress of paying for things you may no longer enjoy becomes magnified". – **SumaCorp**

While the job search is one of the biggest challenges some new immigrants face, acquiring a Canadian credit rating and raising enough cash to get started is another challenge. Without a clear understanding of the Canadian financial system, many new immigrants acquire high-interest consumer loans and credit cards, and when they are unable to pay, their credit worthiness is affected. Some of the major financial institutions are now turning their attention to helping newly-arrived immigrants establish their credit worthiness.

Another mistake some new immigrants make is to quickly use up their available cash to make large purchases like homes or new motor vehicles, or even smaller purchases like household items when other options exist. Depending on your circumstances, you may consider renting rather than buying a home, at least initially, or buying a used vehicle instead of a new one. Explore your options before using up all the money you have.

When it comes to financial institutions, there are alternatives to the "Big Banks" such as credit unions, so make sure to do your research. Also, make an appointment to speak with people at several financial institutions as well as credit counselling agencies to get a better understanding of finance and credit before opening any accounts or obtaining credit.

Disclaimer: The above is for information only and should not be construed as financial advice. Please contact a financial professional for your specific needs.

Finding a Place to Live

Finding a place to live also has its challenges. Most landlords require the standard first and last payment of rent as well as an indication that you will be able to pay your rent for the duration of your lease. It becomes even more challenging since you may not yet have a job that shows stability. In cases like these you will need someone who knows you to act as a guarantor or a character reference; someone who can vouch that you are who you say you are and that you are honest and trustworthy.

In addition to the housing aspect, utility companies (electricity, telephone, cable, gas) also require a guarantor in order for you to enter into a contract with them. If not, they will ask you to pay a very high deposit to secure service. Some have been known to refuse service based on the applicant not meeting the criteria.

Social Insurance Number

You need a **Social Insurance Number** (SIN) to work in Canada. One of the first things you should do after you arrive in Canada is to apply for a **Social Insurance Number** (SIN) for yourself and each member of your family. This number is used to identify you when you work, pay taxes, contribute to pension plans, and use government services. You must have a SIN in order to obtain employment; employers cannot hire you without a Social Insurance Number.

To obtain a SIN, you can apply online or visit a Human Resource and Social Development Centre (HRSDC). Make sure you have at least one piece of identification, preferably your Permanent Resident Card or passport, when applying for your Social Insurance Number.

Health Insurance Coverage

Canada's national health insurance system, often referred to as "Medicare", is one of the best in the world. Medicare is available to all permanent residents and citizens of Canada, and is designed to ensure that all residents have reasonable access to medically necessary hospital and physician services.

Under this system, you don't normally pay directly for most health care services – they are paid through your taxes. The universal standards for Medicare are set by the federal government but each province and territory manages its own health-care program.

To access Medicare, you need a health insurance card and you should apply for one as soon as you arrive in Canada. Each member of your family will need their own health insurance card, even babies.

There are some minor differences in eligibility and services provided from province to province so check with the Ministry of Health in the province in which you settle. For instance, in British Columbia, Ontario, Quebec and New Brunswick, there is a three-month waiting period before your coverage begins. You should buy your own private health insurance in case you need medical care during the waiting period. However, you must do so **within five days of arriving in Ontario**. If you don't, the insurance companies will not provide coverage for you.

Ontario Health Insurance Plan – OHIP

To be eligible under the Ontario Health Insurance Plan (OHIP), you must be a resident of the province. To be considered a resident, for the purpose of obtaining Ontario health insurance coverage, you must:

- hold Canadian citizenship or immigration status
- make your permanent and principal home in Ontario
- be physically present in Ontario for at least 153 days in any 12-month period

In most cases, new and returning residents applying for health coverage must also be physically present in Ontario for 153 of the first 183 days following the date they establish residency in Ontario (a person cannot be away from the province for more than 30 days in the first six months of residency).

Finding a Doctor

Let everyone you meet know that you are looking for a family doctor. It's not very easy to find doctors in Ontario because of a shortage, but some clinics will have signs that state "Accepting New Patients." If not, ask your friends or neighbours to ask their family doctor if they would accept you, or ask others for referrals.

You can visit the website of the College of Physicians and Surgeons of Ontario (**www.cpso.on.ca/Doctor_Search/dr_srch_hm.htm**) to locate a doctor in your area. You can also call 416-967-2606 in Toronto, or 1-800-268-7096 ext 626 in Ontario.

Make sure the doctor you choose fits your needs. Do you want a male or female doctor? Do you want someone who speaks your language? Is the doctor's office close to where you live or where you work? Does the office offer after-hours service?

Additional Health Care Information

In an effort to assist new immigrants whose first language is not English, some hospitals in the Greater Toronto Area have developed programs to make it easier for professionals to provide the best care possible to all patients. Listed below are some of these programs:

St. Michael Hospital in Toronto developed a practical tool for use by doctors, nurses, and other allied health care professionals when they encounter a patient who does not speak English, especially when a translator is not immediately available.

- A Practical Language Translation Aid for Health Care Professionals **www.stmichaelshospital.com/content/translation/translation.asp**

The Ontario Hospital Association developed:
- Your Health Care – Be Involved **www.oha.com/Client/OHA/OHA_LP4W_LND_WebStation.nsf/page/ Your%20Health%20Care%20-%20Be%20Involved**

The Canadian Association for Mental Health (CAMH) has developed the Multilingual Resources section to provide multi-language information on mental health and addiction for people whose first language is not English.
- **www.camh.net/About_Addiction_Mental_Health/Multilingual_Reso urces/multilingual_information_pr.html**

Employment Standards in Ontario

The Employment Standards Act, 2000, known as the ESA, is a law that sets minimum standards for fair workplace practices in Ontario. This Act does not cover employees in federal jurisdiction and persons in a few other special categories. There are exceptions and special rules for some employees.

The following website contains additional information on employment standards in Ontario **www.labour.gov.on.ca/english/es/index.html**. If you live in another province, check with your provincial Ministry of Labour.

Obtaining A Driver's License

Many new immigrants might decide that a motor vehicle is a priority, particularly because of the winter season. As a matter of fact, even if you will not be purchasing a motor vehicle immediately, it is very important for you to obtain a driver's license as it is a very useful piece of identification.

Each province in Canada has its own set of rules with respect to obtaining a driver's license. Therefore, it is recommended that you consult the website of the province within which you choose to reside for specific driver license requirements. The guidelines and requirements for Ontario will be used in this book.

A newcomer to Ontario who holds a driver's license from another province or country can use that licence for a maximum of 60 days, after which he or she is required to apply for an Ontario driver's licence.

Ontario has a two-step Graduating Licensing System (G-Licence) which allows new drivers to gradually gain experience and develop skills. If you are a licensed driver from other Canadian provinces, the United States of America, Japan, Korea, Switzerland, Germany, France, Great Britain or Austria, and you have two or more years of driving experience within the last three years, you may be able to get a full G-licence without taking a knowledge or road test. You must, however, pass a vision test, and show proof of your previous licence and driving experience.

If you are a licensed driver from other countries, with two or more years of driving experience within the last three years, you must pass vision and knowledge tests, and then you'll be issued a G1 licence. If you believe you will be able to pass a G2 test, you can go ahead and arrange a road test. If you are successful, you will have earned full driving privileges. If you are unsuccessful, you will have to arrange for a G1 test.

Applying for an Ontario Driver's Licence

- You must be at least 16 years of age and complete an application.
- If you have previous driving experience, present your out-of-country/province driver's licence verifying previous driving experience or written confirmation about your previous driving experience from the licensing authorities
- Provide one other piece of identification showing your signature
- Pass a vision test
- Pass a knowledge test and a G1 or G2 road test as required
- Pay the applicable fees

The Educational System

Canada has a universal education system that makes it mandatory for children to attend school up to the ages of 15, 16 or 18, depending on the province in which you reside. Tuition is provided free; however, there are incidental costs that your child's school may ask you to pay from time to time. Depending on the country you are coming from, you may be accustomed to schools that are private and fee-based. There are many private and fee-based schools and centres of learning available in Canada, but this section will primarily discuss the public school system.

Government schools, which are called public schools, make up the majority of schools in Canada. Approximately 95 per cent of children attend the Government elementary and secondary schools, which are managed by school boards allocated by districts. Students attend the school nearest to them unless there are special needs such as French Immersion, which is discussed below.

Public District School Boards

The majority of immigrants settle in the Greater Toronto Area in which the two largest school boards in Canada and among the largest in North America are found. These are the Toronto District School Board and the Peel District School Board. Together, these boards serve almost 400,000 students, approximately 40 per cent of whom were born outside Canada.

In fact, so many new immigrants settle in this area that the Peel District School Board has taken the initiative to reach out to the community and offer information that parents want most – in their own language.

The Board has developed a number of websites (www.peel.edu.on.ca/index.asp) in the top 25 languages of Peel Region, including Punjabi, Hindi, Urdu, Arabic, Chinese, Farsi and Spanish. This will enable parents and others whose first language is not English to get the information they need to register their children for school, understand the school system, and assist their children with reading and writing.

Catholic District School Boards

The Catholic schools across Canada are similarly aligned to the public schools and are also administered by boards. The Catholic District School Boards' curriculum is based on the teachings of Christian values; therefore the practice of prayer and worship are held in high regard by the Catholic school system.

If you are settling in the Greater Toronto Area, The Toronto Catholic District School Board and the Dufferin-Peel Catholic District School Board are the two largest boards serving this area, with an enrollment of approximately 180,000 students.

The registration process for the Catholic District School Board is similar to the Public District School Board. The one major difference is that a Baptismal Certificate for the student entering elementary school and for one of the parents must be shown.

French Immersion

The opportunity to learn French in public schools is open to all students when they start Grade 1.

While having your school-age children develop proficiency in Canada's two official languages is a great experience, bear in mind that French Immersion is an option. Sometimes, students find the program quite challenging and opt to enter the regular school system.

Enrolling Your Children in School

To enroll your child in a school, you need to take documents that show proof of age, proof of address as well as immunization and education records. In many cases, immigration documents will be requested. Here is a checklist of requested documents:

- Proof of Age – birth certificate or birth registration card or passport
- Proof of Address – any lease or bills, bank statement or credit card statement
- Immunization Documents
- Immigration documents – permanent resident card or record of landing
- Education Records – recent report cards

Your children's skills in language and mathematics may be tested before they are assigned to a class based on the results of the test.

Your Role as a Parent in the School System

In some countries parents leave all the educational preparations and activities to the school system and to the teachers. However, in Canada, it is expected that parents take an active role in their children's education. There are a number of ways you can do this, some of which we have included here:

- **School Councils**
  Most schools in Ontario have a school council, a support group for students and parents. School councils include parents, school staff, community representatives and students. They offer advice to school principals on a variety of topics.

It is extremely important that you become a part of your child's School Council in order to contribute your expertise and help your child succeed at school. The following websites contain information on how parents can get involved in their children's schools and communities – **www.parentvoiceineducation.org/english/index.html** and **www.edu.gov.on.ca/eng/**

- **Parent-Teacher Interviews**
  These are held to discuss your child's performance in school and are usually scheduled after you receive your child's progress report. It is important to attend these because you are able to talk one-on-one with your child's teachers and ask questions. These interviews are for every child whether or not he or she is struggling in school.

- **Parent Conferences**
  If you have school-age children and are thinking of settling in the Region of Peel (Brampton, Mississauga, Caledon), the Peel District School Board has an annual parent conference that is offered, not only in English and French, but in Cantonese, Mandarin, Vietnamese, Punjabi, and Arabic. This is due, primarily because of the large number of immigrants who settle in the region.

  This initiative provides parents with useful and practical ways to help their children succeed at school. Some of the workshops may include:

  - Build your child's reading skills
  - Discover the fun in science
  - Getting results – help your child prepare for provincial tests
  - Help your child be successful in French immersion
  - Help your child develop good study skills
  - Help your child succeed in math
  - Motivate the reluctant reader
  - Plan for success – help your teen make the right career choice
  - Turn math into family fun
  - Understanding the school system – how to encourage school success.

Public Libraries

Libraries can play a valuable role in your integration into Canadian society and should be one of the first places you visit. Libraries can be found in almost every community in Canada. Some offer services in many different languages. The following link contains information on most libraries in Southern Ontario: **www.library.on.ca/links/libraries/organizations.htm**.

Recreational Facilities

Similar to libraries, every community has recreational facilities, operated by the city, where you and your family can enjoy many free services or pay a small fee for some services. This is an opportunity for you and your family to begin to socialize with and understand other cultures.

Adults can also take part in most of the programs offered at these facilities. Use the yellow pages of your telephone directory to find the nearest location to your home. Visit the facility and observe families taking part in activities.

What Should You Pack When Emigrating?

To make your transition a bit easier, you should consider taking the personal and household effects that you will need to settle quickly. If you have furniture that is in good condition, take it with you. This may mean not having to spend money to purchase new furniture, and saving the money to help to pay rent and purchase basic necessities. You are allowed to ship personal items at a reduced fee. Consult with Customs and Immigration or the Canadian Consulate in your country for details.

SECTION IV

REFERENCES AND RESOURCES

CHAPTER 14

Finding Your Way Around

This section is a listing of resources to assist you in your job search, as well as in your transition to Canada. It is important to note that this is not a complete list as there are many organizations that provide services to support new immigrants all across Canada. Some services overlap; others are standalones. See the Online Resources section for websites and links to other related organizations, including an updated list of organizations that host annual Internationally Educated Professionals Conferences.

Organizations

ACCES Employment Services

ACCES is a community-based organization that has been providing a wide range of professional and integrated employment services to mostly new immigrants since 1986. While it is one of the top organizations for internationally-educated professionals to "access" prior to, and after, they arrive in the Greater Toronto Area, there are three unique programs that deserve special mention and will be of valuable assistance to new immigrants.

There is the **Talk English Café**, where new immigrants whose first language is not English, meet regularly to practice English conversational skills in a relaxed setting. Through informal discussion, interaction with others, and trainer-directed activities, participants practice and improve their English conversational skills. Workplace-related topics are also discussed as participants learn how to communicate in the Canadian workplace. This program has been made possible through TD Bank Financial Group, one of Canada's major banks, and Tim Hortons, a household name for Canadians' morning coffee.

The second program is **Engineering Connections**, a six-week program that provides internationally-trained engineers with essential knowledge and skills to help them connect with employers. Participants learn and practice effective job search strategies, develop an understanding of workplace communication and employer expectations, learn about the engineering labour market in the province and the country at large, and gain important insights on professional engineering standards and professional licensing in Ontario. They also enhance their professional skills through workshops on project management, software for engineers, and Canadian engineering codes and standards.

By the end of the program, participants are able to conduct more focused job searches that target companies looking for candidates with their specific skills, expertise and experience.

The third program, which has garnered an award for excellence, is **Speed Mentoring®.** Speed Mentoring events offer new Canadians an opportunity to meet and network with professionals in their field who provide them with sector-specific and occupation-specific information and advice. It helps them build professional networks, 10 minutes at a time. Speed Mentoring® has been acknowledged in the Globe and Mail as a creative recruitment strategy, and ACCES received a 2007 Minister's Award for Excellence in Service Innovation for Speed Mentoring®.

COSTI Immigrant Services

COSTI Immigrant Services is a community-based multicultural agency that, for more than 50 years, has been providing employment, educational, settlement and social services to all immigrant communities, new Canadians and individuals in need of assistance. (**www.costi.org**).

The agency operates from 20 locations in the Greater Toronto Area and provides services in more than 60 languages. See the resources section for the agency's website.

Community MicroSkills Development Centre

Community MicroSkills Development Centre is a non-profit organization serving the Greater Toronto Area since 1984. They provide settlement, employment and self-employment services to individuals, giving priority to the needs of immigrants, youth, visible minority people, and low-income women.

Their programs focus on developing clients' skills, increasing their information base, and facilitating opportunities for them to transfer their skills and knowledge to the Canadian workforce. (**www.microskills.ca**).

Newcomer Centre of Peel

The Newcomer Centre of Peel (NCP) is a leader in settlement and integration services within the Region of Peel, supporting newcomer families in their settlement process. (**www.ncpeel.ca**)

Peel Newcomer Strategy Group

Peel Newcomer Strategy Group (PNSG) is a new organization designed to develop a coordinated and integrated settlement services model to ensure the successful settlement and integration of immigrants into all aspects of community life in the Region of Peel. (**www.peelnewcomer.org**).

Skills Without Borders

Skills Without Borders (SWB) is a Brampton Board of Trade project aimed at "connecting employers and skilled immigrants". Its main objective is to raise awareness among local employers of the Business Case for Diversity, i.e., the impact on the bottom line of recruiting and managing a culturally-diverse workforce. The project has conducted labour market research as well as research on employers' barriers to hiring skilled immigrants. SWB has published two resource guides for employers.

In partnership with settlement agencies, SWB organizes and delivers presentations to both employers and skilled immigrants to reduce employment barriers and prejudice and, ultimately, help employers find the skills they need for business growth and development while immigrants gain employment in their field of training and expertise. (**www.skillswithoutborders.com**).

HireImmigrants.ca

Hireimmigrants.ca is a part of Toronto Region Immigrant Employment Council (TRIEC), and provides employers with the tools and resources they need to better recruit, retain and promote skilled immigrants. (**www.hireimmigrants.ca**).

Hire Immigrants Ottawa

Hire Immigrants Ottawa (HIO) is a community-based initiative that brings together employers, immigrant agencies and stakeholders to enhance employers' ability to access the talents of skilled immigrants in the Ottawa area. (**www.hireimmigrantsottawa.ca**).

PROJAM

PROJAM (Progressive Jamaicans Association of Canada) is a non-profit organization fostering the settlement, integration and networking of new newcomers/immigrants and their families into the Canadian society through information and education. Through their eLink (electronic based) service they provide members with on-going timely and relevant information such as job postings, education, financial and lifestyle matters, which are important to their settlement and integration.

S.U.C.C.E.S.S (United Chinese Community Enrichment Social Service).

S.U.C.C.E.S.S. was founded in 1973 as a non-profit charitable organization and is now one of the largest social service and immigration service providers in British Columbia. Its mandate is to assist immigrants to overcome language and cultural barriers, and to empower newcomers to become fully participating and contributing members of the Canadian society.

More recently, S.U.C.C.E.S.S Employment Services, with funding from the Canada-British Columbia Labour Market Development Agreement, has developed a framework/model and toolkit to support cultural diversity initiatives within the workplace. This multi-dimensional toolkit provides organizations with numerous supports and options for customizable diversity interventions. (**www.embracingdiversity.ca**). Another resourceful website based in British Columbia is **Diversity at Work (www.diversityatwork.ca**).

DiversiPro

Although DiversiPro Inc. does not work directly with new immigrants, it benefits newcomers through its training and management consulting services for organizations across the country. They work with companies, assisting them to develop practices that help newcomers to be recruited and supported in the workplace. Their mission is to help organizations succeed in being reflective, responsive and relevant to the changing markets and communities they serve. (**www.diversipro.com**).

Engineering Matching and Placement Program (E-MAP)

This program was established in 2006, and is based in British Columbia and provides job-matching services for internationally trained engineers (ITEs), connecting them with manufacturing firms in the province. The program was developed by the Canadian Manufacturers & Exporters and the Society of Internationally Trained Engineers of British Columbia (SITE BC).

Online Resources

The organizations and websites mentioned below are for information purposes only and do not represent all the resources available; therefore, you are urged to conduct independent research for additional information.

Care has been taken to make sure that, up to the time of writing, the websites listed below were operational. Because of the changing nature of the Internet, it is possible that some sites may no longer be functional by the time this book reaches your hands.

Accounting Services & Associations

- CGA Canada
  www.cga-online.org

- Canadian Institute of Chartered Accountants
  www.cica.ca

- Certified General Accountants of Ontario
  www.cga-ontario.org

- Certified Management Accountants of Ontario
  www.cma-ontario.org/

- Chartered Accountants e-career Map
  www.ecareermaps.ca/en/ca/index.html

- Institute of Management Accountants
  www.imanet.org

- The Canadian Academic Accounting Association
  www.caaa.ca

- The Institute of Chartered Accountants of Ontario
  www.icao.on.ca

Bridging & Mentoring Programs

- Access And Options For Foreign-Trained Health Care Professionals (Medical Radiation & Medical Laboratory Science Technologies, Respiratory Therapy)
  www.michener.ca/access/

- Access to Baccalaureate Nursing Preparation (York University)
  www.yorku.ca/web/futurestudents/programs/template.asp?id=615

- Bridging for Internationally Educated Nurses (Mohawk College)
  www.mohawkcollege.ca/discover/ce/health/bien.html

- Bridging for Green Careers
  www.senecac.on.ca/fulltime/BGC.html

- Bridging to University Nursing for Internationally-Educated Nurses (Centennial College)
  www.centennialcollege.ca/rpnbridginghybrid
- Career Bridge
  www.careerbridge.ca/
- Career Edge
  www.overview.careeredge.ca/
- Creating Access To Regulated Employment (CARE) For Nurses
  www.care4nurses.org/
- Health Informatics And Financial Services Bridging Project: George Brown Computer Programmer
  www.immigrantnet.com/Pages/CIRN%20Career%20Help%20Programs. asp
- Information and Communications Technology Council
  www.ictc-ctic.ca/
- International Massage Therapy Bridging Programme (IMTBP)
  www.cmto.com/
- International Midwives Pre-Registration Program (Access To Midwifery Pre-Registration Program)
  www.ryerson.ca/ce/midwife/
- International Optometric Bridging Program (University of Waterloo)
  www.optometry.uwaterloo.ca/iobp
- Internationally Educated Dietitians Pre-registration Program (IDPP)
  www.ce-online.ryerson.ca/ce/
- Ministry of Citizenship & Immigration, Government of Ontario
  www.citizenship.gov.on.ca/
- Preparation for Registration for Foreign-Trained Medical Laboratory Technologists
  www.mohawkcollege.ca
- The Veterinary Skills Training & Enhancement Program (VSTEP)
  www.vstepontario.org
- Three Choices: New Options For Foreign-Trained Nurses Seeking Employment In Ontario (Ottawa)
  www.algonquincollege.com/HealthAndCommunity/hs_programs/f_t_n .htm
- Toronto Region Immigrant Employment Council
  www.triec.ca
- Vitesse Bridging Program For Foreign-Trained Biotechnology Professionals (Ottawa)
  www.vitesse.ca/programs/vbp.asp

Career Development & Job Search Services

- ACCES Employment Services
  www.accestrain.com

- CanadiaNurse.com
  www.canadianurse.com

- Career Professionals of Canada
  www.careerprocanada.ca

- Charity Village
  www.charityvillage.ca/cv/nonpr/nonpr3.html

- COSTI Employment Services
  www.costi.org

- Job Bank
  www.jobbank.gc.ca

- JobsEtc.
  www.jobsetc.gc.ca

- Newcomer Centre of Peel
  www.ncpeel.ca

- Progress Career Planning Institute
  www.pcpi.ca

- Skills for Change
  www.skillsforchange.org

- Work Placement Programs – Newcomer Opportunities for Work Experience Program (NOW)
  www.tdsb.on.ca

Practice Firms

- Canadian Practice Firm Network
  www.rcee-cpfn.ca/

- Experica
  www.experica.ca

- Canadart
  www.canadart.ca

- Reboot Canada
  www.rebootcanada.ca/

Credential Assessment Standards & Services

- Canadian Association of Medical Radiation Technologists
  www.camrt.ca/

- Canadian Information Centre for International Credentials
  www.cicic.ca

- International Credential Assessment Service of Canada
  www.icascanada.ca

- International Credential Evaluation Service (ICES)
  www.bcit.ca/ices/

- International Qualifications Assessment Service (IQAS)
  http://employment.alberta.ca/immigration/4512.html

- Ontario Regulators for Access
  www.regulators4access.ca

- Service des évaluations comparatives d'études (SECE)
  www.immigration-quebec.gouv.qc.ca

- University of Toronto Comparative Education Services
  www.adm.utoronto.ca/

- World Education Services
  www.wes.org

Education & Training

- Association Des Enseignantes et des Enseignants Franco-Ontariens
  www.franco.ca/aefo/
- Association of Universities and Colleges of Canada
  www.aucc.ca
- Association of Canadian Community Colleges
  www.accc.ca/
- Canadian Association of University Schools of Nursing
  www.causn.org
- Canadian Teachers' Federation
  www.ctf-fce.ca/
- Centre for Education and Training
  www.tcet.com
- Educational Programs Innovation Centre – EPIC
  www.epic-edu.com/
- Ministry of Training, Colleges and Universities
  www.edu.gov.on.ca/eng/
- Ontario College of Teachers
  www.oct.ca/IET/?lang=en-CA

- Ontario Institute for Studies in Education
  www.oise.utoronto.ca

- Ontario Secondary School Teachers' Federation
  www.osstf.on.ca

- Ottawa WorldSkills
  www.ottawa-worldskills.org

Engineering Associations

- Aerospace Industries Association of Canada
  www.aiac.ca

- Alliance of Technology and Science Specialists of Toronto
  www.atss.org

- American Society of Civil Engineers
  www.asc.org

- Association of Consulting Engineers of Canada
  www.acec.ca

- Association of Professional Geoscientists of Ontario
  www.apgo.net/

- Canadian Academy of Engineering
  www.acad-eng-gen.ca

- Canadian Aeronautics and Space Institute
  www.casi.ca

- Canadian Council of Professional Engineers
  www.ccpe.ca

- Canadian Council of Technicians and Technologists
  www.cctt.ca/

- Canadian Institute of Mining, Metallurgy and Petroleum
  www.cim.org

- Canadian Society for Chemical Engineering
  www.chemeng.ca

- Canadian Society for Civil Engineering
  www.csce.ca

- Canadian Society of Industrial Engineers
  www.mie.utoronto.ca

- Canadian Society for Mechanical Engineering
  www.csme-scgm.ca/

- Canadian Society of Safety Engineering
  www.csse.org/

- Canadian Technical Employment Network
  www.cten.ca

- Consulting Engineers of Ontario
  www.ceo.on.ca/

- Engineering Institute of Canada (EIC)
  www.eic-ici.ca

- Geological Association of Canada
  www.gac.ca

- International Consulting Engineering Federation
  www.fidic.org

- Institute of Electrical and Electronics Engineers Canada
  www.ieee.ca
  www.toronto.ieee.ca

- Institute of Industrial Engineers
  www.iienet.org

- Municipal Engineers Association
  www.municipalengineers.on.ca

- Natural Sciences and Engineering Research Council of Canada
  www.nserc.ca

- Ontario Association of Certified Engineering Technicians and Technologists
  www.oacett.org

- Ontario Environment Industry Association
  www.oneia.ca

- Ontario Network of International Professionals Online
  www.onip.ca

- Ontario Society of Professional Engineers
  www.ospe.on.ca

- Professional Engineers of Ontario
  www.peo.on.ca

- Society of Manufacturing Engineers
  www.sme.org

- The Canadian Coalition of Women in Engineering, Science, Trades and Technology
  www.ccwest.org

- The Canadian Society for Chemistry
  www.chemistry.ca

- The Chemical Institute of Canada – CIC
  www.cheminst.ca

- The Ontario Association of Architects
  www.oaa.on.ca

Government Departments/Agencies

- A Guide for Foreign Trained Industrial Mechanics (Millwrights)
  www.edu.gov.on.ca/eng/training/foreign.html
- Canada International
  www.canadainternational.gc.ca
- Canadian Space Agency –CSA
  www.space.gc.ca
- Citizenship and Immigration Canada, Government of Canada
  www.cic.gc.ca
- EmploymentOntario
  www.edu.gov.on.ca/eng/tcu/employmentontario/
- Human Resources & Social Development Canada
  www.hrsdc.gc.ca
- Institute for Aerospace Research
  www.iar-ira.nrc-cnrc.gc.ca
- Labour Market Information
  www.labourmarketinformation.ca
- Ministry of Health and Long Term Care, Government of Ontario
  www.health.gov.on.ca
- National Research Council of Canada – NRC
  www.nrc-cnrc.gc.ca
- Ontario Immigration
  www.OntarioImmigration.ca
- Ontario Ministry of Education
  www.edu.gov.on.ca/

Health Care

- Academy of Applied Pharmaceutical Sciences
  www.aaps.ca
- Association of International Physicians and Surgeons of Ontario
  www.aipso.ca
- Canadian Association for Clinical Microbiology and Infectious Diseases
  www.cacmid.ca
- Canadian Association of Critical Care Nurses
  www.caccn.ca

- Canadian Association of Occupational Therapists
  www.caot.ca

- Canadian Association of Radiologists
  www.car.ca

- Canadian Association of Registered Diagnostic Ultrasound Professionals
  www.cardup.org

- Canadian Centre for Occupational Health and Safety
  www.ccohs.ca

- Canadian Association of Medical Radiation Technologists
  www.camrt.ca

- Canadian Association of University Schools of Nursing
  www.causn.org

- Canadian College for Naturopathic Medicine
  www.ccnm.edu/

- Canadian Dental Association
  www.cda-adc.ca

- Canadian Lipid Nurse Network
  www.lipidnurse.ca

- Canadian Nursing Information
  www.nursingindex.com

- Canadian Physiotherapy Association
  www.physiotherapy.ca/jobsearch.asp

- Canadian Society of Pharmaceutical Scientists
  www.csps.ca

- Canadian Student Nursing Association
  www.cnsa.ca

- Cancer Care Ontario
  www.cancercare.on.ca/

- Care for Nurses
  www.care4nurses.org

- College of Audiologists and Speech-Language Pathologists of Ontario
  www.caslpo.com/

- College of Medical Radiation Technologists of Ontario
  www.cmrto.org

- Eldercare Home Health Inc.
  www.eldercarehomehealth.com

- Health Professions Regulatory Advisory Council
  www.hprac.org

- International Medical Graduates (IMG) Ontario
  www.imgo.ca

- International Pharmacy Graduate Program
  www.ipgcanada.ca
- International Pharmacy Graduate (IPG Program – Toronto, Waterloo, Ottawa)
  www.newontariopharmacists.com/IPG
- Ontario Association of Medical Radiation Technologists
  www.oamrt.on.ca
- Ontario College of Homeopathic Medicine
  www.ochm.ca
- Ontario College of Pharmacists
  www.ocpinfo.com/
- Ontario Hospital Association
  www.oha.com
- Ontario Medical Association
  www.oma.org
- Ontario Nurses' Association
  www.ona.org
- Ontario Nurses Association
  www.cna-aiic.ca/cna
- Ontario Pharmacists Association
  www.opatoday.com
- Pharmacy Examination Board of Canada
  www.pebc.ca
- Registered Practical Nurses Association of Ontario
  www.rpnao.org
- Registered Nurses Association of Ontario
  www.rnao.org
- The College of Nurses of Ontario
  www.cno.org
- The International Council of Nurses
  www.icn.ch
- The Royal College of Physicians and Surgeons of Canada
  www.rcpsc.medical.org
- Toronto Institute of Pharmaceutical Technology
  www.tipt.com
- University Health Network
  www.uhn.ca
- Volunteer Order of Nurses
  www.von.ca

- Your Health Care – Be Involved - Created by the Ontario Hospital
  Association's Patient Safety Support Service
  www.oha.com

References/Referrals

- 211 Toronto
  www.211toronto.ca

- Canada InfoNet
  www.canadainfonet.org

- FindHelp Information Services
  www.findhelp.ca

- Job Search Guide
- **www.jobsearchguide.ca/**

- Multicultural Inter-Agency of Peel

  www.miag.ca/

- Professional Networks for Immigrants
  **www.settlement.org/sys/faqs_detail.asp?k=WORK_CUL&faq_id=40013
  52**

- Ontario WorkInfoNet
  www.on.workinfonet.ca/

- The Environmental Education Directory
  www.enviroeducation.com
  www.envirodirectory.on.ca

- WebCPA
  www.webcpa.com

- Work Destinations
  www.workdestinations.org

- WorkInfoNet
  www.workinfonet.ca

Other Professional Associations

- Association of Ontario Land Surveyors
  www.aols.org
- College of Chiropodists of Ontario
  www.cocoo.on.ca
- College of Chiropractors of Ontario
  www.cco.on.ca
- College of Dental Hygienists of Ontario
  www.cdho.org

- College of Dental Technologists of Ontario
  www.cdto.ca
- College of Denturists of Ontario
  www.denturists-cdo.com
- College of Medical Laboratory Technologists of Ontario
  www.cmlto.com
- College of Midwives of Ontario
  www.cmo.on.ca
- College of Occupational Therapists of Ontario
  www.coto.org
- College of Opticians of Ontario
  www.coptont.org
- College of Optometrists of Ontario
  www.collegeoptom.on.ca
- College of Physiotherapists of Ontario
  www.collegept.org/
- College of Physicians and Surgeons of Ontario
  www.cpso.on.ca
- College of Psychologists of Ontario
  www.cpo.on.ca
- College of Respiratory Therapists of Ontario
  www.crto.on.ca
- College of Veterinarians of Ontario
  www.cvo.org/
- Law Society of Upper Canada
  www.lsuc.on.ca
- Ontario Professional Foresters Association
  www.opfa.on.ca
- Ontario College of Social Workers & Social Service Workers
  www.ocswssw.org
- Real Estate Council of Ontario
  www.reco.on.ca
- Registered Insurance Brokers of Ontario
  www.ribo.com
- Royal College of Dental Surgeons of Ontario
  www.rcdso.org

Resources for Older Workers

Please note that not all of these are Canadian websites, neither do they all cater exclusively to older workers, but they provide enough useful information that warrants their inclusion.

- Age Advantage
  www.ageadvantage.ca
- Dinosaur-Exchange
  www.dinosaur-exchange.com
- Experience Works
  www.experienceworks.ca/
- Fifty-Plus/CARP
  www.50plus.com & **www.carp.ca**
- Halton and Peel Professional Executive Network
  www.happen.ca
- Prime 50
  prime50.com
- Retired Brains
  www.retiredbrains.com
- Senior Job Bank
  www.seniorjobbank.com

Self-Employment

- Business Start-up Assistant (Starting a Business in Canada)
  www.bsa.cbsc.org/gol/bsa/site.nsf/en/su06889.html
- Enterprise Toronto
  www.enterprisetoronto.com/
- Small Business Enterprise Centre (Brampton)
  www.brampton-business.com/
- Microskills Community Programs & Services
  www.microskills.ca/
- Mississauga Small Business Enterprise Centre
  www.mississauga.ca/portal/business/startingabusiness
- Job Skills
  www.jobskills.org

Settlement Programs

- Centre for Foreign Trained Professionals and Trades-people
  www.cftpt.org
- COSTI
  www.costi.org

- Immigration Peel
  www.immigrationpeel.ca
- Microskills Community Programs & Services
  www.microskills.ca/
- Newcomer Centre of Peel
  www.ncpeel.org
- OCASI
  www.ocasi.org
- Peel Newcomer Strategy Group
  www.peelnewcomer.org
- Professional Jamaicans Association
  www.projam.org
- Settlement.org
  www.settlement.org
- S.U.C.C.E.S.S. (United Chinese Community Enrichment Social Service)
  www.success.bc.ca/
- YMCA Toronto Newcomer information Centre
  http://www.ymcatoronto.org/

Internationally Educated Professionals Conference Organizations

- Global Talent
  www.globaltalent.ca/
- Immigrant Employment Council of British Columbia
  www.iecbc.ca
- Internationally Educated Professionals
  www.iep.ca
- Kithener-Waterloo Multicultural Centre
  www.kwmc.on.ca/
- London-Middlesex Immigrant Council
  www.lmiec.ca/
- Niagara Immigrant Employment Council
  www.niec.ca
- Ottawa Job Match Network
  www.ottawa-worldskills.org/
- Skills International
  www.skillsinternational.ca/
- Waterloo Immigrant Employment Network
  www.wrien.com
- Working in Nova Scotia (WINS)
  www.workinginnovascotia.ca/

Short List of Staffing/Employment Agencies/Recruiters

- Accountemps
  www.accountemps.com

- Bilingual Source
  www.bilingualsource.com

- Buckley Search Inc.

- **www.buckleysearch.com/**

- Find a Recruiter
  www.findarecruiter.com/

- Employers Choice
  www.theemployerschoice.com/en/index.htm

- Health Employment Solutions
  www.medconnexions.ca

- Headhunters Directory
  www.employmentagencies.ca/headhunters_recruiters/Ontario/Toronto8.htm

- Officeteam
  www.officeteam.com

- PTC Accounting
  www.ptcaccounting.com

- Robert Half International
  www.rhi.com

- TopNotch Executive Staffing
  www.topnotchstaff.com

Canadian Job Boards

The following is a sample of Canadian job boards that provide career information to job seekers. Some allow you to post your résumé and search for job vacancies. The Job Bank is the official job board maintained by the Government of Canada and allows free résumé posting services to Canadian job seekers and employers.

- All Star Jobs
  www.allstarjobs.ca
- Career Beacon
  www.careerbeacon.com
- Career Owl
  www.careerowl.ca
- Higher Bracket
  www.higherbracket.ca
- Job Boom
  www.jobboom.com
- Job Bank
  www.jobbank.gc.ca
- Monster.ca
  www.monster.ca
- TorontoJobs.ca
  www.TorontoJobs.ca
- Workopolis
  www.workopolis.ca
- WowJobs
  www.wowjobs.ca
- Yahoo! Hot Jobs Canada
  www.ca.hotjobs.yahoo.com

Bibliography

The following is a list of books that were consulted while writing this book, and by listing them here, I am paying tribute to their authors.

- 60 Seconds & You are Hired, *Robin Ryan*

- Best Canadian Résumés, *Sharon Graham*

- Boost Your Interview IQ, *Carole Martin*

- Career Distinction, William Arruda & Kirsten Dixson

- Guerrilla Marketing for Job Hunters, *Jay Conrad Levinson, & David E. Perry*

- How to Choose the Right Person for the Right Job Every Time, *Lori Davila and Louise Kursmark*

- Human Rights at Work, published by *Human Resources Professionals of Ontario in partnership with Ontario Human Rights Commission.*

- Interview Fitness Training, *Carole Martin*

- Job Search Magic, *Susan Britton Whitcomb*

- Outwitting the Job Market, *Chandra Prasad*

- The Career Counselor's Handbook, *Richard Bolles & Howard Figler*

- The Complete Job Search Guide for Latinos, *Murray A. Mann and Rose Mary Bombela-Tobias*

- The Hard Truth About Soft Skills, *Peggy Klaus*

- The Insider's Guide to Career Coaching, *Marcia Bench*

- The Power of Positive Thinking, *Dr. Norman Vincent Peale*

- Use Your Head to Get Your Foot in the Door, *Harvey MacKay*

- What Color is Your Parachute, *Richard Bolles*

APPENDICES

Appendix I: Résumé, Cover Letter and Thank-you letter Samples
Chronological Résumé #1

NORMA PHILLIPS-GORE
578 Tankerville Drive, Brooklin, ON L1T 3B4
905·555·0000 Email: npg@xxxx.ca

CAREER PROFILE

A short chronological résumé with historical timelines of work experience.

EXECUTIVE ASSISTANT
Confident ■ *Self-Motivated* ■ *Professional*

A confident and professional Executive Assistant with strong written and verbal communication skills, offering 8+ years of progressive experience providing high-level and efficient administrative support to senior executives. Comfortable interacting with officials of high profile organizations and government departments. An excellent team player who is self-motivated and pro-active and who anticipates the needs of the team and adapts readily to the demands of the job. Exceptionally well-organized, able to handle multiple priorities and manage time effectively. Proficient with MS Word, Excel, PowerPoint, Access and Outlook and the Internet. Adept at generating and compiling correspondence.

PROFESSIONAL EXPERIENCE

Executive Assistant **SBEC Credit Union, Toronto ON** **Sept 1998 – Present**

Selected from a pool of 12 candidates to provide executive support to the senior management team of this local member-driven credit union with 80 staff and over $400 million in assets.
- Plan, coordinate and prioritize daily workload to meet deadlines, and hold weekly meetings with 3-member administrative team to brainstorm ideas on how to streamline processes and build a cohesive team.
- Creatively use PowerPoint in developing marketing materials such as brochures, presentations and special reports".
- Attend senior management meetings; take, transcribe and disseminate minutes quickly and accurately for appropriate actions and follow-ups.
- Prepare, compose, format and type confidential correspondence and proofread same to ensure accuracy and compliance with Bank standards.
- Update records regularly and prepare weekly and monthly staff and management absenteeism reports using Access and Excel.
- Receive visitors, respond to telephone, email and in-person enquiries, take messages and/or refer calls to appropriate department or personnel.

Office Manager **Holiday Suites, Halifax, NS** **Feb 1996 – Aug 1998**

Offered full time employment as **Front Desk Administrative Assistant** after completion of a 4-month co-op placement and promoted to Office Manager after 2 years. Excelled at turning "cold callers" into guests.
- Acted as Marketing Manager for 3 months during incumbent's absence. Planned and organized 4 very successful conferences attended by an average of 300 people at each event.
- Supervised administrative assistant and receptionist and oversaw all A/R and A/P responsibilities.
- Developed excellent customer/vendor relationships and earned numerous employee awards for "going beyond the call".
- Managed a 20-line Meridian Phone system; fielded incoming calls and answered questions about services, and provided exceptional customer service.
- Processed credit card, cash and Interac payments and handled refunds quickly and accurately.

EDUCATION & PROFESSIONAL DEVELOPMENT

Hospitality Management Certificate, Best Eastern University (1995)
Executive Administration Diploma, Atlantic College (1994)
Short courses: Supervisory Techniques, Customer Service Excellence & Effective Selling

Functional Résumé

DEEPAK DeSOUSA
1221 Broker Street
Bramalea, ON L6P 2Y7

Tel: (905) 555-0000
Cell: (416) 555-0000
Email: **ndesousa@xxxx.com**

PROFESSIONAL PROFILE

Résumé short list
of functional skills.

Highly skilled, well-rounded **Automotive Manager** with excellent interpersonal, communication and leadership skills seeking to broaden skills base and have full responsibility for a medium-sized trucking company. Core strengths include:

✓ Administration   ✓ Communication   ✓ Leadership

PROFESSIONAL EXPERIENCE

Five years' experience as the "Jack of all trades and master of all" in this family-run trucking business. Previously owned and managed small auto repair shop.

Administration
✓ Took charge of all administrative responsibilities associated with business startups.
✓ Assumed bookkeeping and payroll responsibilities after incumbent resigned suddenly; recruited and trained replacement within 6 weeks.
✓ Sat on recruiting panel for all licensed mechanics and labourers hired at the company.

Communication
✓ Create brochures, flyers and presentation materials for marketing purposes.
✓ Presenter at trucking symposium in Lansing, Michigan (2005).
✓ Spokesperson for company on all issues of a public nature including resolution of complaints and misunderstandings.

Leadership
✓ Member of 4-person senior management team that oversees business operations.
✓ Elected as 2nd Vice President of All-City Trucking Association, a 200-strong membership organization providing education and advocacy for its members.
✓ Currently serving as VP of Membership for the Speedy-Wheel Toastmasters Club.

WORK HISTORY

✓ Khan-nali Trucking Company   Mississauga, ON   2001 – Present
✓ River Oaks Auto Repairs   Brampton, ON   1998 - 2001

PROFESSIONAL QUALIFICATIONS

✓ Small Business Management Certificate, Entrepreneurship Institute (2003)
✓ Graduate of the **Truck and Coach Mechanic Apprenticeship** Program, New College, Toronto (2001).
✓ Mechanical Engineering Degree, University of Madras

Combination / Hybrid Résumé

GLORIA TAYLOR

Tel: 506·420·0000

5 Garibaldi Street, Fredericton, NB E3V 1Y3

QUALIFICATION SUMMARY

- ▶ Skilled in counselling individuals on a one-on-one basis or in group sessions.
- ▶ Strong communication and interpersonal skills with evidence of working harmoniously with people from diverse backgrounds and social sectors.
- ▶ Analyzed, identified, investigated and reported on problems, opportunities and solutions during co-op placement.
- ▶ Researched and developed a **Handbook of Community Resources** based on various presentations, visits and meetings.
- ▶ An excellent team player...always offered to assist supervisor with projects in order to meet critical deadlines.

RELATED EXPERIENCES

This is a simple combination résumé for someone with limited experience in social work. The résumé starts with a qualification summary highlighting her skills as they relate to the job posting. It also shows an amended version of her work history in chronological order and including some functional skills.

- ▶ Through work/study program and volunteerism exposed to a broad range of social service programs:
  - • Help for Families With Children
  - • Child Abuse Crisis Intervention Services
  - • Mediation & Conflict Resolution Services
- ▶ **Teaching**
  - • Taught lessons in reading, comprehension, spelling and mathematics in a private school setting.
  - • Developed curriculum for Day Camp and prepared and participated in activities for children ages 4 to 11.
  - • Volunteered at public school and supervised students on school trips.
- ▶ **Counselling**
  - • Counselled individuals via telephone and at community shelters.
  - • Provided a "listening ear" to seniors in nursing homes.

HISTORY

HONEYMOONER'S GETAWAY, Niagara Falls   1994 – 2002
- ▶ Hired as **Office Manager** for a busy Bed & Breakfast business. Honed skills in:
  - • **Budgeting**... prepared monthly cash-flow statements monitored budget and controlled expenses.
  - • **Administration**...coordinated all administrative functions including Payroll and ordering office supplies.
  - • **Bookkeeping**... ensured entries made to general ledger were accurate and valid; scrutinized accounting sheets and cheques before forwarding for approval.

EDUCATION & TRAINING

- ▶ **Meridian College**, Toronto, ON   2006
  - • *Social Service Worker Diploma*
  - • *Crisis Prevention Certificate*
- ▶ **Bloor Park Institute**, Niagara Falls, ON   1994
  - • Business Management Certificate

Sample Résumé of a Former Senior Executive

This client had recently retired from his high-powered job, but wanted to continue working. He thought his age and former titles were going to pose a challenge, so we worked together to develop this simple one page résumé that de-emphasized his title and downplayed much of his accomplishments.

A. CARL THOMAS

158 Anytown Drive
Brampton, ON
L0Z 3T7
Telephone: (905) 000-0000

> This former senior executive wanted to continue working, but did not want the stress of his former position. We decided to use a résumé that highlighted only the functional skill areas mentioned in the job posting.

SUMMARY OF QUALIFICATIONS

- Extremely competent professional with 10+ years of successful experience in data centre management, systems development and telecommunications.

- Outstanding **Communicator**. Commended for having strong interpersonal and analytical skills in relating with others, resolving conflicts and identifying and solving problems.

- Excellent **Management** skills. Project management experience includes designing, planning and prioritizing all facets of data processing projects to enhance efficiency and productivity. Directly accountable for the administration of a **$16 million** budget. Managed data processing/information systems for operations in both North America and Europe.

- Effective **Planning and Organization** skills. Known as a strategist. Well organized, meticulous, and adept at taking projects from the concept stage to successful implementation.

- Exceptional **Supervisor**. Supervised between **80** and **200** employees at various stages of career. Motivated staff to increase efficiency, productivity and quality of service year-over year.

- Strong record in negotiating hardware and software contracts ranging in value from **$250,000** to **$2.2 million**.

- Coordinated opening of new data centre/head office complex totalling over **50,000** sq. ft.

CAREER HISTORY

2002 - Present	**Anytown Corporation**, Mississauga, Ontario *Management Consultant*
1999 - 2002	**ABC Facilities Management Company**, Birmingham, England *Director of Data Centres and Computing Services*
1996 - 1999	**The Data Services Corporation**, San Diego, CA *Director of Management Information Systems for North America*

EDUCATION

MBA, York University, Toronto
BA, American University, Iowa

A Sample Cover Letter

JENNIFER JAMES
57 Regina Drive
Vancouver, BC V26 1A2
Telephone: (250) 555-1002   jennjames@xxxxx.ca

March 8, 2009

Mr. Harry Evans
Human Resources Manager
Vancouver National Bank
Western Bank Plaza
Vancouver, BC V7T 2T2

Dear Mr. Evans:

I noticed on the Career Opportunities page of your website that you are looking to hire a Human Resources Manager who has "*highly developed communication skills, superior interpersonal skills and the ability to deliver feedback, motivate others and handle conflict situations in a proactive manner*". I am attaching my résumé for consideration as I believe your requirements closely match my background.

For more than 7 years I was the HR Manager of ABC Bank, a subsidiary of a major Canadian Bank. I led the team that recruited, selected and trained all employees for the Call Centre, had direct responsibility for 20 full and part-time employees and was recognized by the bank for providing exemplary leadership and demonstrating a positive attitude and team spirit. I conducted employee evaluations, provided feedback, encouraged innovation and developed a "customer first" initiative which was adopted across the organization.

I have an MBA from the Masters University, a certificate in Human Resource Management from Nova College, and completed a variety of supervisory and management courses. I have excellent interpersonal and time management skills and implemented an "employee first" initiative which reduced staff turnover in the department from 30% to 10% within the first three months on the job. I earned the President's "Pioneer Award" for this initiative.

I would welcome an opportunity to join your team and continue my track record of developing people. Please call me at (250) 555-1002 to set up a time for us to meet.

Sincerely,

Jennifer James

Enclosure

Thank-You Letter

JENNIFER JAMES
57 Regina Drive
Vancouver, BC V26 1A2
Telephone: (250) 555-1002   jennjames@xxxxx.ca

March 8, 2009

Mr. Harry Evans
Human Resources Manager
Vancouver National Bank
Western Bank Plaza
Vancouver, BC V7T 2T2

Dear Mr. Evans:

Thank you for meeting with me yesterday to discuss the goals you have for your Call Centre. I left the interview with a clearer understanding of the challenges you face, and I am quite keen to join your staff.

As I indicated to you, I was hired by my former company to resolve some of the same staff turnover issues and within three months of joining the organization and implementing a "small team" concept, the turnover rate decreased from 35% to 10%. We found out that the employees felt disconnected from the organization and lacked the motivation to work to the level of their capabilities. I am confident I have the ability to reduce the turnover rate in the department.

Thanks, once again, for sharing your time with me, and I look forward to hearing from you next week Thursday as you indicated.

Sincerely,

Jennifer James

Appendix II: Top 20 Interview Questions

In a 2010 survey by The Wright Career Solution, Canadian recruiters, HR professionals and hiring managers were asked to list their top 5 interview questions. Listed below are 20 of the more common questions cited by the 192 respondents. To help you practice for interviews, develop answers to these questions:

1. What do you know about our company (as well as what differentiates us from the competition)?

2. What do you know about the position?

3. Describe your ideal role? For example, if you could tailor a position to suit your skills & interests, what would it look like?

4. Describe three accomplishments that saved money, increased revenue, improved quality?

5. What has been your best achievement to date and how did you accomplish it?

6. What benefits would I be getting if I hired you into this position?

7. Tell me about your experience and how it has prepared you for this position?

8. How would your peers, subordinates, manager or previous employer(s) describe you?

9. What do you think are your opportunities for development?

10. What skills do you possess that could use some fine-tuning?

11. Based on your experience and skills, how do you feel you can add value to this position/role?

12. What did you do to prepare for this interview?

13. Why do you want to work for this company?

14. Walk me through the steps of a project you successfully completed.

15. What do you feel would be a weakness if we hired you?

16. Tell me about a time you worked with someone you did not like or vice versa. What was the situation and outcome?

17. How will we know you are the right choice?

18. What positive personal attributes do you bring to the job?

19. Why are you interested in this job?

20. Why do you want to leave (or why did you leave) your present (last) company?

Appendix III: Résumé Advice for Internationally-Educated Professionals

Below is a list of answers to the question: *"If you had one piece of résumé advice for someone who is an internationally-educated professional or new immigrant, what would it be?"* Please note that we have tried to accommodate as many answers as possible and you because of that you may notice some repetitions:

- Focus on your skills as they relate to the job you are applying for

- Proper spelling and grammar are imperative. Employers want to know that those representing them can maintain their professional image.

- Provide more detailed information on former employers and the positions held. Provide relevant website addresses for background information.

- Highlight Canadian equivalency in your education and use a functional résumé format

- Align work experience with the job requirements

- Be specific and detailed about job experience and capabilities

- Have the résumé professionally done if necessary

- Get your education accredited for equivalence at **www.icas.com**

- Ensure your education/qualifications have been accredited by a Canadian institution - and not just for 'immigration' purposes

- Make sure your résumé clearly addresses all the qualifications of the position. Adding a cover letter with a table (Column 1: You asked for; Column 2: I have) is very helpful to a recruiter who has hundreds of résumés to go through

- Don't put personal details, e.g. date of birth, place of birth, marital status, etc.

- Try to gain volunteer Canadian experience to boost your chances

- Find out the most current way to send résumés

- Familiarize yourself with best practices of North American résumé writing, i.e., no personal information, picture, etc.

- Have the education assessed against Canadian standards, for example, a CA in India is equivalent to Canadian CGA Level 4

- Target contract roles to gain Canadian experience

- Summarize job related skills in the first paragraph of your résumé

- Get professional assistance

- Make it simple and easy to read...not too wordy

- Be honest

- Link your experience to Canadian needs

- Show your draft documents to lots of your friends and acquaintances. Take the feedback seriously. Do it until you get a version that is error free

- Have recommendation letters

- Match your past job responsibilities with the appropriate Canadian title. Give details of your work experience and of the education (possible equivalence). Provide a Profile or summary to enlist skills and accentuate transferable skills. If English/ French is not your mother tongue go to a centre and get proof reading assistance

- Clearly indicate the "Canadian equivalent" of the education achieved overseas

- Tailor résumé to position, and research, research, research

- Detail as much Canadian experience as possible, even if it's part-time, volunteer, or short-term work. Also, point out Canadian similarities in any relevant prior experience

- Create and grow a network - and don't ever stop!

- Know who you are applying to. Customize résumé and research the employer

- Provide brief comparison of international standards vs Canadian: ISO, Lean, Manufacturing, etc.

- Highlight how you were the top producer, how you solved problems, etc. This would show that you were an above average employee and that's impressive no matter where you came from

- Seek professional assistance developing a résumé suitable for North American roles

- List skills and ability and what you can bring to the table

- Enrol in courses at your local post-secondary educational institution to understand the Canadian HR methods so you may meet the standards for professional accreditation

- Use the combination résumé style and obtain a Canadian certification in the field that you are seeking to pursue before seeking work in Canada

Appendix IV: Résumé Pet Peeves

(As reported in a Survey of Recruiters & Hiring Managers)

The phrase "pet peeve" means small things that tend to annoy or frustrate someone. The question: *What's your #1 Pet Peeve* was asked to generate a list of petty annoyances that hiring managers have regarding résumés and job seekers should be aware of before sending their résumés. Here is a list of some of the more common ones:

- Get to the point. Too wordy; makes it hard to figure out what the person has done and how it applies to current application
- When they have a different position listed on their résumé than their cover letter
- Redundancies
- When tasks/duties performed are listed in paragraph form
- Pictures on résumés
- Vague or general objectives, summaries
- Lack of professionalism in the layout and composition
- Not formatted to flow nicely, sometimes bullets are all over the place and it makes them hard to read. After going through 100s of résumés, these are the ones that test one's patience
- Massive email blasts where the résumé does not target the position they are applying for
- Chronological history of events dating back to high school (especially when the applicant has been out of high school for 3 or more years).
- Content that is unrelated to the role!
- I do not like to see the standard "responsible for" beginning of each point regarding experience. I also do not care to see "references available upon request". Of course they would be!
- When résumé is longer than three pages
- People don't write to the posting requirements.
- Résumé not specific to position applied for
- "Generic" Objectives
- Formatting and font issues
- Résumé addressed to the wrong company or person in the letter, but has the correct email information. Also, sending out the same résumé to everyone.
- When the résumé very obviously does not match the job
- We are an industry specific recruiting firm. We are not interested in receiving résumés from candidates with no relevant experience in this industry. Do not waste people's time.

- Ones that come across as 'help me, I need a job'. I am quite willing to hire them if their skills fit my needs; their job is to make that connection for me if they want the job
- Lack of detail on duties and accomplishments
- Résumé or cover letter not addressing the requirements of the position
- Lack of thought and planning that goes into a presentation
- Very long résumés – eight + pages. No matter how many years of experience a person has - this is too much and no one is really reading all that! Plus, do not confuse a résumé with a portfolio! I like seeing portfolios, but at the interview, or if requested.
- Person does not succinctly explain what exactly they have done in each position and qualifying who these employers are.
- Dull job descriptive statements – simply listing their normal daily routine! Need S.T.A.R Statements- Situation, Task, Action & Results
- Too generic. Lots of 'Responsible fors' with few real accomplishments
- Disorganization
- Terrible formatting
- Talking about "being responsible" for things without including related quantitative objectives and results
- Résumés longer than two pages, and messy
- Using a font that is hard to read
- People who arbitrarily apply for a job, without indicating why we should hire them and why they want the opportunity.
- Too much information to sift through - start with summary statement
- People who cut and paste and have a number of different fonts, etc. on the same document
- When people include irrelevant information
- Résumés not tailored to the specific position.
- When information is left out or information on the résumé is inaccurate.
- Applying for positions they are not even remotely qualified for. They are just applying for everything they see. This occurs more times than not.
- Lack of customization, grammar and spelling/formatting errors
- Not sending a chronological résumé
- I strongly dislike receiving unsolicited résumés.
- Poor structure/layout
- Too much fluff

LIST OF CONTRIBUTORS

Heather Chetwynd, MES, TESL
Voice to Word Consulting Inc.
Toronto, ON
E-mail: heather@voicetoword.ca
Website: **www.voicetoword.ca**
Phone: 416-535-8869

Paul Copcutt
Square Peg
Dundas, ON
Email: **paul@paulcopcutt.com**
Website: **www.paulcopcutt.com**
Phone: 905-628-1100

Sue Edwards, PCC, CHRP
Development by Design
Carlisle, ON
Email: **sue@development-by-design.com**
Websites: **www.development-by-design.com**
www.clearingthe90dayhurdle.com
Phone: 905-690-0456

Lydia Fernandes, BA, TESL, CPBS
Motivode
Toronto, ON
Email: **Lydia@motivmode.com**
Website: **www.motivmode.com**
Phone: 905-495-0582

Sharon Graham, MCRS, MCIS, MCCS,
CPRW, CEIP
Graham Management Group
Milton, ON
Email: **info@grahammanagement.com**
Website: **www.grahammanagement.com**
Phone: 866-622-1464

Wayne Pagani, MCRS, MCIS, MCCS
W.P. Consulting & Associates
Ontario
Email: **developcareers@gmail.com** /
cwpagani@rogers.com
Website: **www.developcareers.ca**
Phone: 613-526-1982

Susan Guarneri, CMBS, COIMS, NCCC,
CCMC, MRW, MCC
Susan Guarneri Associates
Three Lakes, WI 54562
E-mail: Susan@AssessmentGoddess.com
Website:
www.AssessmentGoddess.com
Phone: 715.546.4449

Susan Joyce, MBA
NETability Inc.
Marlborough, MA 01752-0507
Email: **sjoyce@netability.com**
Website: **www.Job-Hunt.org**
Phone: 508-624-6261

Maureen McCann, BA, MCRS, MCIS,
MCCS
ProMotion Career Solutions
Ottawa, ON
Email: **Maureen@mypromotion.ca**
Website: **www.mypromotion.ca**
Phone: 613-721-8646

Dr. Roberta A. Neault, CCC, RRP,
GCDFi, CCDP
Life Strategies Ltd.
Aldergrove, BC, V4W 4A4
Email: roberta@lifestrategies.ca
Website: **www.lifestrategies.ca**
Phone: 604-856-2386

Ingrid Norrish
Small Business Marketing Coach &
Event Producer
Creative Meeting & Marketing Services
Email: **info@ingridnorrish.ca**
Website: **www.ingridnorrish.ca**
Phone: 905-456-0438

Tanya Sinclair, CHRP, MCRS
TNT Human Resource
Management
Pickering, ON
Email: **info@tntresumewriter.com**
Website: **www.tntresumewriter.com**
Phone: 416-887-5819

Cecile Peterkin, PCC
Cosmic Coaching Centre
Toronto, ON
Email: **Cecile@cosmiccoachingcentre.com**
Website: **www.cosmiccoachingcentre.com**
Phone: 416-782-5001

Lynda Reeves, BA, MCRS
Added Value Résumés
Ontario
Email: **addedvalue@rogers.com**
Website:
www.linkedin.com/in/LyndaMargaret

Wanda Marsman
Assistant Manager
COSTI Immigrant Services

Dorothy Wright, BA, TESL
The Wright Number
Toronto, ON
Email: thewrightnumber@gmail.com
Website: **www.diwright.com**
Phone: 416-208-3982

Janet Barclay
Organized Assistant
Hamilton, ON
Email: **janet@organizedassistant.com**
Website: **www.organizedassistant.com**

Phone: 905-538-1044

Denise Ricketts-Goombs, RN, MPH,
MBA,
Wellington, Florida

The career professionals listed above have years of experience in their respective fields. All have earned distinguishing professional credentials, which are explained below:

BA	—	Bachelor of Arts
CCC	—	Canadian Certified Counsellor
CCDP	—	Certified Career Development Practitioner
CCM	—	Credentialed Career Manager
CCMC	—	Certified Career Management Coach
CEIP	—	Certified Employment Interview Professional
CHRP	—	Certified Human Resource Professional
CMBS	—	Certified Master Branding Strategist
COIMS	—	Certified Online Identity Management Strategist
CPBS	—	Certified Personal Branding Strategist
CPRW	—	Certified Professional Résumé Writer
CRS	—	Certified Résumé Strategist
GCDFi	—	Global Career Development Facilitator Instructor (Master Trainer)
MBA	—	Master of Business Administration
MCC	—	Master Career Counselor
MCCS	—	Master Certified Career Strategist
MCIS	—	Master Certified Interview Strategist
MCRS	—	Master Certified Résumé Strategist
MES	—	Master of Environmental Studies

MRW	—	Master Resume Writer
NCCC	—	National Certified Career Counselor
PCC	—	Professional Certified Coach
RRP	—	Registered Rehabilitation Professional
TESL	—	Teacher of English as a Second Language

About the Author

Daisy Wright, BA, CCMC, CCM, CCDP, CRS

DAISY is a multi-award winning Certified Career Management Coach and has gained a reputation as one of Canada's top career and employment strategists. Through her company, **The Wright Career Solution**, she offers job search and career coaching to mid- to senior-level professionals as well as to internationally-educated professionals.

As a result of writing this innovative book, she has received recognition and endorsement from organizations, government officials and other Canadian career leaders. For two years, she was the Career Advisor to CBC **The Link**, a Radio Canada International program.

Her corporate work experience began in Jamaica, and a year and a half with the United Nations in New York contributed significantly to her ability to understand and work with people from a variety of cultures. In Canada she worked in banking and manufacturing environments before launching her business. She honed her training and facilitation skills as an instructor in the Executive Administration program at Sheridan College.

In addition to this book, she has had samples of her work published in several of the more popular résumé, cover letter and career books, including **Twitter Job Search Guide**, **Interview Magic**, **Best Canadian Résumés**, **Expert Résumés for Baby Boomers, Résumés for the Rest of Us, Quick Résumé & Cover Letter Guide, Same-Day Résumé, No Nonsense Job Interviews**, and **No Nonsense Cover Letters**. She has also been featured in the career coach section of the college text book, **Business Communication: Process & Product**. Daisy has been quoted in the Globe & Mail, Toronto Star, Brampton Guardian, Share Newspaper, Caribbean Camera, Job Boom, South Asian Focus, and the Australian Career Development Magazine.

Daisy is a founding member of Career Professionals of Canada, and as a result of her work supporting the Canadian career industry, she was twice awarded the organization's highest recognition, Outstanding Canadian Career Leader. She is a member of Career Directors International and Women in Ecommerce (WECAI).

She holds a BA in Public Administration from Ryerson University, a Post-graduate Diploma in Career Development from Conestoga College and was recognized by the College with the **2011 Alumni of Distinction** award. In addition, she is a Certified Career Management Coach, Credentialed Career Manager and Certified Résumé Strategist.

Daisy has been a mentor with The Mentoring Partnership and The United Achievers Club of Brampton, and was nominated for a 2011 Zonta Women of Achievement award by the Brampton-Caledon Chapter of Zonta International.

BRING US TO YOUR NEXT EVENT

Daisy Wright is available as a career coach, keynote speaker and workshop facilitator on various topics, particularly as they relate to internationally educated professionals. For details on her services for groups or individuals, please visit:

Website: **www.thewrightcareer.com**
Email: **info@thewrightcareer.com**
Phone: 647-930-4763

For individuals interested in cost-effective career coaching, visit our Coaching Club at **www.careertips2go.com**. Daisy consults with internationally educated professionals looking for assistance in understanding and navigating the Canadian job search maze and getting hired faster. Visit **www.nceinstitute.com**, or send an email to **author@nceinstitute.com**.

Ask us about the **Business Writing Basics** course offered through NCE Institute. It is designed for individuals or staff members who write letters, memos and emails and need a refresher on some elements of writing, word usage and spelling.

Index

84

questions, 60, 66–66, 72, 121, 221

panel type, 61

parent-teacher, 188

portfolios, 71, 226

preparation, 60, 72–73, 96, 104, 154

punctuality, 62, 73, 117, 164

reference checks, 74

reference list, 77

restaurant type, 62

self-promotion, 59–60

telephone type, 60

thank-you letters, 72, 73

traditional type, 61

victorious attitude, 26

weaving passions into, 35

Islaih, Khaled, 140–141

J

Jain, Shifali, 137

"James", 151–152

"Jin", 147–148

job aggregators, 100

job boards

aggregators, 100

LinkedIn, 98

niche boards, 96

professional groups, 93

résumés, 96, 102

web sources, 211

job fairs, 91–92, 158

job interviews. *See* interviews

job leads. *See* leads

job shadowing, 119, 126

journaling, 82, 119, 127

Joyce, Susan, 96–97, 101–102, 229

K

"Kally", 148–149

Kaputa, Catherine, 49

keywords, 45, 122

L

labour market

barriers, 111

staying competitive, 35

diversity, 196

engineering, 193

internships, 104

strengthening links to, 36

research into, 138, 177, 195

web sources, 203

language training

CBC, 170

clear speech tips, 169–171

ESL 168–169

French immersion, 186, 187, 188

S.U.C.C.E.S.S, 150, 196

Talk English Cafe, 193

web sources, 164, 204

layoffs, 126–127

leads

following up, 58, 96

job fairs, 92

networking, 81, 108

sharing, 117

libraries, 94, 106, 170, 188, 189

LinkedIn, 39, 76, 85, 92, 96, 97,98–99

See also social media

listening

The Art of War, 143

once hired, 79

in interviews, 60, 61

language training, 168, 170

to news shows, 126

as skill, 87, 96, 124–126

smiling as aid, 60

teleconference calls, 56

voicemail, 120, 125

Love, Alaina, 35–36

M

Mankletow, James, 20

Mann, Murray, 67, 212

marketing. *See also* networking;
résumés; social media

books on, 212

branding, 39, 52

consulting checklist, 108–110

practice firms, 113

references, 75

self-marketing, 30,39, 40,
131, 133

Marsh, Mr., 132–133

Martin, Carole, 59, 73, 212

McCann, Maureen, 23–27, 100, 229

Medicare, 182

mentoring

Career Bridge, 104–105, 139

ELT, 168–169

The Mentoring Partnership,
105, 137, 139

seeking out mentors, 156,
159

Speed Mentoring, 194

S.U.C.C.E.S.S, 149–150

web sources, 197

Microsoft, 89

Millard, Nancy, 180

mistakes

cover letters, 46

financial, 181

interviews, 61, 73, 155

in job searching, 120–121

language, 171

motivation

career assessment, 29, 37

goal setting, 20

networking, 97

possibility thinkers, 119

self-employment, 107

as soft skill, 116

"Muhammad", 144–145

multilingualism

as commodity for senior–level
positions, 83

as an asset, 98, 164, 167

library services in multi–
languages, 188

COSTI Immigrant Services,
194

mental health information in
multi–languages, 184

schooling information in
multi–languages, 186

Myers–Briggs Type Indicator (MTBI),
30, 37

N

Ndububa, Edward, 136–137

NCP (Newcomer Centre of Peel), 194,
199, 209

Neault, Roberta, 107, 229

negativity

abandoning, 21, 28

ANTs, 118

branding, 49–51

stress, 23, 27

networking. *See also* social media

ABCs, 93–95

B2B, 107

calling cards, 55, 92

through your community,
106, 144

209